Break-Up Survival

I Lost Him
but
I Found Myself

FLORENCE CHOW

Note: All the names (except the author's) associated with the events mentioned in this book have been altered. Any resemblance to actual persons, locales, or events is purely coincidental.

Contact:

E-mail: breakupsurvivalbook@gmail.com

Having survived your break-up,

you will realize

how much stronger and wiser you have grown!

CONTENTS

The Reason I Wrote This Book

i) My Break-Up as the Beginning

A break-up is like the flu—medicine may not cure it, but time will heal it. It feels awful, but hold on! It just takes a little longer. Be patient. You will eventually recover and grow much stronger, and may even become immune to heartbreak.

This is the advice I would give my friends when they whined to me about their break-ups. To be honest, though, I learned the hard way that it was easier to say these words than to live by them. While going through my own break-up, I found out just how destructive it could be to part from someone with whom I had developed such a deep connection. My emotional crisis brought on an overwhelming bitterness that enslaved me. I fell into a spiral of countless sleepless nights during which I thought a lot about myself, my life, and the meaning of living in this world. During the darkest moments soon after my break-up, inspired by my chaotic feelings, I wrote a few songs and their background stories, which became the starting point of this book.

Following my break-up, I felt ashamed. It hurt not only my heart, but also my ego. I was upset with myself, but only with myself, and with no one else. I was sad about my stupidity and mad at my irrationality. I thought, "I'm a strong person; I'm well-educated; I always pay my own bills; I stay healthy and fit; I'm a decent person ... Now, why should I be heartbroken because one man won't continue to see me? There are so many single men out there. What's the point of being so attached to him? How can I be so foolish? What's wrong with me?"

1

After having time to review my broken relationship objectively, I began to tell myself, "It's OK if you do not feel all right. Intelligent scientists, successful entrepreneurs, strong athletes ... all sorts of capable people deal with emotional crises, too. You're just one of millions. You're made of flesh and blood, not cold stone, so you have feelings. You don't have to blame yourself; you should just be kind to yourself."

This break-up led me to severe grief, yet also stimulated me to live the life I aspired to have. Instead of remaining frustrated and negative, I endeavored to optimize myself—I persevered in fitness class and strengthened my body; I made sizable progress in my career through my dedication and time management skills; and, most importantly, I recorded my unforgettable experience in music and words, which was incredibly fulfilling.

Eventually, I defeated my heartbreak using my secret weapons. One year after my break-up, I unveiled the upgraded version of myself.

I lost myself when I was with him.

I then lost him, but I found myself.

Pondering my break-up, I realized that many of the economic and financial principles I had learned in school and the working world could be applied to emotional situations as well. Viewing my emotional avalanche from this rational perspective helped me walk through the sadness and then successfully rebound. My feelings evolved from shock, to a sense of betrayal, to depression, and then, finally, to relief. Defeating this heartbreak was a triumph for me. Recognizing how these experiences and thoughts had enabled me to recover from the break-up, I decided to share my methodology with you to assist you in your journey.

ii)   Understanding Other Types of Break-Ups

Besides parting with a lover, other types of separations may also lead to heartache. Therefore, the term "break-up" in this book refers not only to the end of a romantic relationship, but also to many other types of "goodbyes," including:

- The termination of relationships with family members, friends, employers/employees, and/or business partners
- The loss of a loved one
- The loss of something important (such as a skill, one's health, one's youth, etc.)
- Moving out of one's comfort zone

There are different goodbyes I have said and will say to different parties throughout my entire life, before the last "Goodbye!" I will eventually hear from this world.

iii)   What I Want to Offer You in This Book

Here, I honestly share my experiences and perceptions to inspire, enlighten, and entertain you. I sincerely hope that my feelings will resonate with you.

Break-ups are similar to perfect storms. They can demolish one's life unexpectedly and cruelly. They may occur several times throughout one's life—very likely between adolescence and middle age, but also at other stages. My heart and soul have grown stronger from every emotional challenge. After surviving this unforgettable crisis caused by ending my relationship with my ex, I am now able to manage my emotional issues much better than I did before. In many situations in daily life, work, and study, one's emotional intelligence, known as "emotional quotient" (EQ), has a greater impact than cognitive intelligence, known as "intelligence quotient" (IQ), in terms of solving a problem.

Challenge and opportunity have an interesting relationship—very often, crisis gives rise to growth. To memorialize my break-up, I wrote a few songs and then this book, which became souvenirs of my failed love story. While I was writing this book, I worried about what my family and friends would say about me behind my back. I wondered, "Will they judge me for disclosing my private pain?" Despite such concerns, I decided to express my opinions openly because I place greater value on benefiting others by sharing my experience than on what people think of me. Offering you this book is like *making my secret diary public*.

This book will bring you a mixture of feelings—sadness, bitterness, empathy, and delight, as well as inspiration. This work is not exactly soul-healing chicken soup; it is more like spirit-boosting **spicy chili chowder**. Some of my readers found this content blunt, while others finished reading and felt encouraged, like seeing fresh green leaves in the spring following a long, cold winter.

I also wish to take this opportunity to motivate you to write whenever you are facing a difficult situation. It is not only a course of writing and creating, but also a process of logical reasoning, because you think a lot while you are writing, reviewing, and revising. Very likely, by the time you finish turning your thoughts into words, your problem will be solved.

Break-ups are never easy. It takes strength and patience to get through them. However, after overcoming one, you will realize how much stronger and wiser you have grown.

My hope is that my experiences and insights here will be your companion as you walk through the darkness and then welcome the sunrise, enjoy the fresh breeze, and smile in bliss.

From a broken heart to a resilient soul,

*may **Break-Up Survival***

accompany you through your emotional crisis.

Part One   Understanding the Break-Up

Chapter I   Ending the Relationship

1.   Remember Me

I wrote the song "Remember Me" during my most heartbroken time, the first week after I found out what my ex had been hiding from me. The moment I realized what had happened, I began shedding tears. My whole body felt torn apart. With great sorrow, I made a decision for myself:

"He and I are over."

With all the struggles in my mind, my final thought was "Although we are no longer together, all I can hope for is that you will **remember me**."

It was the end of our history. It was the start of this book, which arose from my emotional landslide.

Remember Me

You and me, our story
Long history but ends up here

I know you're moving on with life
I know things are moving on in life
I know you will wish me all the best

*Will you still remember me? (like you had a dream)
*Will you sometimes talk to me? (like you still love me)
*I wish that happy you will always be
*Will you still remember me?

I feel lost, fallen apart
This is life and I'll be strong

I know we're heading down different ways
I know our lives have already changed
I know you will wish me all the best

*Will you still remember me? (like you had a dream)
*Will you sometimes talk to me? (like you still love me)
*I wish that happy you will always be
*Will you still remember me?

The city is the same, but you are different
I wonder when I will see you again
One day in the future, when we are older
Maybe I'll see you again, see you again

*Will you still remember me? (like you had a dream)
*Will you sometimes talk to me? (like you still love me)
*I wish that happy you will always be
*Will you still remember me?

2. Logic vs. Emotion

Have you ever experienced a disastrous emotional moment? I have.

I will never forget how I collapsed the morning I saw the pictures of my ex with someone else on social media and realized that he had been hiding his dating status from me for months. I felt like throwing up. My skin was burning. The whole day, I did not want to eat or talk, but I still pretended to be all right in front of everyone at my office. Finally, I got home and broke down in front of the mirror. It felt as though my heart was being clawed by a savage monster. My mind exploded. A part of me somehow still could not believe what had happened. That night, I could not fall asleep at all, even though I was exhausted after having worked all day.

My sleeplessness continued for three days. No matter where I was or what I was doing, I felt frustrated. My energy had been completely sucked out of my body. I felt isolated—as if the rest of the world was moving forward without me.

Due to my lack of sleep, I came down with a horrible case of the flu; my throat burned incessantly and my body was racked by a violent cough. For a week, as I was struggling with insomnia, I clearly heard my heartbeat and felt pressure in my chest. I had the sensation that my heart was beating with effort, and I genuinely worried that it might stop beating entirely. Even when I managed to fall asleep, I woke up every few hours from a nightmare in which my ex appeared. Above all else, his uninvited presence in my mind kept haunting me. The sadness, the sickness, and the fatigue struck me down and totally trapped me.

Meanwhile, the respective logical and emotional sides of my mind were fighting a fierce battle. *Logically*, I was trying to convince myself to see this as an excellent opportunity for me to restart my life without him, but *emotionally*, I could not stop myself from thinking about him.

My logical side said to me triumphantly: "Don't you remember how he used you and disrespected you in those days? His personality makes him so difficult to get along with. His behavior let you down so many times. Congratulations! All that is over now. You do NOT have to waste your time anymore. New life, new vision!"

However, my emotional side was still inexplicably attached to him. My memories of us were devastating. The places we had been, the food we had enjoyed, the games we had played, the movies we had watched, the music we had listened to, the gifts he had given me ... all these recollections kept attacking me like bullets.

To escape, I moved away from our old neighborhood; I stayed away from our mutual friends; I went out to meet new people; I listened to other types of music; I changed my diet; I cut my hair short. If I could have created an invention, I would have made a memory-deleting machine to erase all the images of him from my brain and start my life over. I yearned to walk out of the darkness.

Not only did my break-up sucker punch me emotionally and physically, it also caused my attitude toward life to shift from positive to passive.

I told myself: "I am not going to love anyone ever again."

My mind was engulfed in pessimistic ideas:

Nothing lasts forever.

Everything will come to an end.

Anything can change anytime.

The hardest thing for me to genuinely accept was that he and I could no longer be the way we were before. Still, I kept telling myself, "As long as my life is not over, it's OK that the relationship is over."

Meanwhile, I tried to comfort myself by extending my unconditional love with the thought: "If he is happy, I should just be happy for him. Maybe, ten or twenty years from now, he will come back to me."

What was ironic to me was that being an independent woman, the rationale of benefiting from this break-up could not mitigate the impact of my emotional crash. I had to admit to myself that I was a loser at this point, which made me feel ashamed of myself.

I criticized myself for feeling this way: "As I have been living my life as an aspiring businesswoman, I have received higher education, I'm in a decent profession, I'm NOT desperate, but now I am insane because of a disabled romance! How unreasonable I have become. Why am I so frustrated over one guy? What's wrong with me? Why am I humiliating myself?"

I debated with myself: "Excuse me, even a very capable person can be heartbroken at some point because the emotional part of the brain does not operate like the rest of it. We have affection, sentiment, and empathy. These are the gifts human beings have that distinguish us from animals. Be kind to yourself."

I did not want to yield to my emotional turmoil, but having no choice, I understood that only time could heal my wounds. I believed that one day in the future, when I looked back on this, I would surely laugh at my old self's ridiculousness.

During the first month following my break-up, I was completely overwhelmed. The video "If They Left You - Watch This" by Jay Shetty, an inspirational speaker and social media influencer, rescued me. In the video, Mr. Shetty explains:

"Even at your best, you will never be right for the wrong person, but even at your worst, the right person will remind you of your worth. That's the test."

So, I should not construe losing someone who was wrong for me as a loss, but rather as a GAIN.

To prevent myself from doing anything irrational, I kept reminding myself, "As long as you're still alive, everything stands a chance! Hold on and be patient!"

I consoled myself by repeatedly thinking: "The combat between rationality and emotion is an unavoidable process in a break-up. I cannot deny it; I cannot hide away; I cannot lie to myself. After I get through this tough time, I will become a victorious survivor!"

My logical side was relieved while my emotional side crumbled.

Logic versus emotion—which side will finally win?

*Have you defeated an emotional crisis?

----

3. Between Pride and Modesty

I lost him.

At this point, I had to admit my weakness.

I never blamed him.

There was no one else to blame in this world but myself. Now, I had to lay down my crown of pride. This was one of only a few times in my life where I confessed to myself that I had made a mistake.

My ego had to surrender.

I have always been a self-critical person. I set strict rules for myself. I endeavor to achieve my goals. I never want to let anyone down. As a perfectionist, I do not easily allow myself to err or misbehave. "I'm sorry!" is the last sentence I want to hear myself say.

However, this time, I genuinely let myself down. It was the regret deep inside me. If I could go back in time, I would do things differently to avoid this doomed relationship. I had known that my ex and I would not have a future, but I was not strong enough to pull myself out of that obsession with him. This disappointment was torturing me.

In the beginning, I did not want to tell anyone about my shameful emotional crisis, but keeping this to myself made me feel like I was suffocating. After a month, and with a great deal of courage, I decided to talk to a few reliable friends. To avoid embarrassment, I confided in only three friends during my vulnerable time: one elder friend, one childhood friend, and one relationship advisor—wise people, who were not mutual friends of my ex's. They were good listeners. Without judging my ex or me, they gave their objective opinions and shared their own stories about past relationships. They provided me with the confidence to get through this frustrating time. They reminded me of my value. Sharing my feelings with trustworthy friends was an effective way to soothe myself.

Putting aside my pride to acknowledge the fact that I had lost the relationship was the first step toward moving on.

4.   Learning from My Mistakes

You do not love me and that is fine, but you cannot stop me from loving you.

I understood that there was no right or wrong in a relationship, but just that the relationship could move forward or end. Even though he hurt my feelings, it did not mean that he did anything wrong. Dating him might be my mistake, but leaving me was not his fault.

My world shattered when he left me. I had never imagined that his absence could bring me such misery. How much I longed for a pleasant day like before. Inspired by this wish, I wrote the song "Beautiful Day."

Beautiful Day

Blue sky and green grass
Sunshine on my water glass
My mind takes a break today
I am lying on the ground

Music flowing around me
Would you come and sing a song with me
Fresh air swirling around me
Would you join me love me and stay with me

*Hooo it's a beautiful day
*Beautiful day, my beautiful day (enjoy the breeze with me)
*Beautiful day, my beautiful day (let your pet dance with ease)

Music comes in, sing it with me
I will let you dance
Music comes in, sing it with me
I will let you shine
Let me sing this

*Hooo it's a beautiful day
*Beautiful day, my beautiful day (enjoy the breeze with me)
*Beautiful day, my beautiful day (let your pet dance with ease)

A beautiful day always welcomes you.
A beautiful day always belongs to you.

This song sounds delightful, doesn't it? It is funny that I wrote it at my lowest point, during the first month following my break-up. Here, I wanted to reflect the idea that although life made me feel awful, I still wanted to have a beautiful day.

In my grief, I wrote these original lines in the lyrics:

Missing something, missing someone
This is what's in life
Losing something, losing someone,
I just want to cry

It was so pessimistic that I teared up when I sang it to my music producer.

Then, I decided to make it a totally happy song instead, because I hoped to get away from negativity. Therefore, I changed the majority of the lyrics. That sad verse was changed to:

Music comes in, sing it with me
I will let you dance
Music comes in, sing it with me
I will let you shine

The magic of a song is that the lyrics and melody together create a very powerful effect on both the singers and the listeners. This is why I appreciate songwriting. I can express myself through words, and a song can be easily shared and enjoyed by everyone, everywhere.

The best times during the months following my devastating break-up were the hours I spent at the recording studio of an experienced music producer, Eric, in Santa Monica, California. I found that focusing on creative work eased my sadness. Being so productive that we could sketch out a song in just one afternoon bolstered my morale. Additionally, his co-workers at the studio encouraged me after hearing the songs we produced. I found a source of true happiness there. For two months, I went there to write and record songs once a week. That was the place where I rescued myself.

I was grateful that my failures and the lessons I had learned had built the foundation for my new life. Instead of crying and complaining, why not make use of them and let them be my momentum?

As I mentioned before, in many situations, EQ has a greater effect than IQ when dealing with everyday issues. I think one of the most important abilities of a high EQ is:

Letting go.

When I am confronted with stress, my biggest problem is sleeplessness, which causes terrible consequences, including low energy and inefficiency. Being able to control one's emotional condition is essential when it comes to handling challenges in daily life. We are not born with this capability; we develop it with practice over time.

When you record your feelings and thoughts through writing, you feel motivated because you are creating something for yourself. For example, collecting a set of notions, sentiments, or feelings in written form, such as in a song, a poem, a journal entry, or even a book, will boost your joy to new levels. A song actually presents a story, or a group of thoughts, integrated with emotion. Try writing something when you have a special moment, and you will be rewarded with a nice surprise!

As a sentimental person, hoping to end the relationship nicely, I wrote a final letter to my ex (I drafted it when I was on my way home after work in a taxi, shedding tears, feeling completely disconnected from the city's buzzing energy). I openly expressed my heart in a polite tone. The letter ended with:

"I hope you remember the time when we were together.

Thank you for everything you taught me."

Maybe he was not meant to be my companion forever, but he was the one who was sent to teach me a lesson. If it were not my ex, it could have been other men who let me experience similar setbacks.

Why did he leave me? I answered myself, "To look at it objectively, I cannot give him what he wants. Yet, his departure may just be temporary."

I should have been aware of what I lacked and what I needed to improve upon. I had not yet reached my best self. This break-up was a hard knock to me, but instead of beating me down, it drove me to refine myself. **Fury was my fuel.**

In the first month following my dreadful break-up, I was struggling. I wondered, "Should I go meet some new guys at bars or clubs to have some fun as a painkiller?" This would have been the quickest way to lessen the pain. However, would I want to turn myself into a "good girl gone bad"?

I thought about this again and again, and I stopped myself again and again! I told myself:

"He doesn't care about you anymore. Grow up! Why would you destroy yourself by hanging out with random guys? You won't get real happiness from any fling and you may expose yourself to the risks of disease and physical danger.

"Just pretend that you never knew him! You should hang out with someone because you want to, not because you are forcing yourself to. You should do things for your own sake, not as a result of someone else's negative impact. Be strong, and you will overcome this sooner or later! Just like you had a fever and then it went away, you will get over this break-up eventually!"

Although I did not have a fling with any man, I did go out a lot to meet new people. Many men I met asked me to go out on dates with them. They gave me plenty of compliments. Actually, I was disappointed with myself that I did not care for any of them. They were nice people, but I was just not attracted to them. I tried to comfort myself: "If I do not have feelings for them, it is OK. It is not my fault. I do not have to compel myself to date a man. I should be wiser now. I cannot allow myself to make another mistake. If they're kind people, just stay friends with them."

Two months after the break-up, I had a final conversation with my ex at a coffee shop (this is elaborated in Section 21 (One Last Conversation) of Chapter IV (What Have I Done Wrong?)). That was the first and last honest conversation I had with him. He never apologized. Before we parted ways, he suggested that I meet someone new by going to a bar or restaurant.

What I learned from this:

Do not expect any sympathy from anyone.

From here, I closed the door on my past and embarked on my new journey.

*Have you learned something from your relationship(s)?

Chapter II   Reborn

5.   A Little Imaginary Funeral for Myself

Life is one long process comprised of many phases, just like a book with multiple chapters. A story will eventually come to its end. I should appreciate it with a round of applause.

To convince myself to accept the break-up more easily, I tried to come up with a fictitious assumption that this unsuccessful relationship would have jeopardized my life. Therefore, letting it go would have been the only way to rescue myself. I asked myself:

If I were forced to choose between the following two hypothetical scenarios:

1) The break-up never happened, BUT this relationship would cause me a life-threatening misfortune

OR

2) The break-up occurred and it ruined my life, BUT I would have the chance to come back to life after surviving this heartbreak

Which one would I pick?

Of course, I would choose #2, to have a second chance at life rather than deal with a fatal issue! That is the point! Give myself a chance for rebirth!

One night, I made up my mind to bury the past for good. So, I held an imaginary funeral for myself, alone, as a symbol of discarding the former relationship:

I scattered white flowers across my bed. After powering off my phone and other electronic devices, I took a shower, donned a white silk gown, and doused myself with *Chanel Chance*, my favorite perfume. I polished off a generous glass of Cabernet Sauvignon, and lay down quietly.

I had been suffering from severe sleep deprivation for over a month. I was utterly exhausted. I decided, "If I can just fall asleep tonight, it will be the end of this disaster."

I told myself:

"If I wake up tomorrow with the sun, I will be reborn. If I don't wake up, my life will be over. This world will continue as it should, with or without me. Losing my life is the last thing I would ever want to happen, so I should appreciate that I am given the chance to wake up every morning!

"After this funeral tonight, my life will be renewed, so I should live it to the fullest with a smile, starting tomorrow!

"I have lost him, but I have NOT lost this world.

"This world never gives up on me, so why should I lose faith in myself?"

Hence, I provided myself with an affirmation to regain my confidence to finally break free from the jaws of the break-up.

After my imaginary funeral, I felt as if my body and soul had been rebuilt. Having survived the darkness of that night, I saw sunlight and heard birds singing in the morning. I came back to life!

*Are you ready for a new life?

----

6. Renaissance After a Fright

In order to cover up my agony with intense physical sensations, I took a ride on a thrilling roller coaster.

Before I went on that roller coaster, I hesitated, as it looked really scary to me. I told myself, "You will overcome this. Consider it a challenge of life or death. After this, you will come back to life and nothing will be able to defeat you!"

In those three minutes on the roller coaster, I did not think about my ex or anything else. I was too frightened to worry about anything. One single idea took hold in my mind: "I want to continue to live!"

When I got off the roller coaster, my legs were shaking, but I felt thrilled. I had not been that relaxed in a long time! It felt as though the heavy gray cloud above my head had cleared. My world seemed more colorful than before.

There were ups and downs on the roller coaster, just like in my life. In fact, the lower points of my life give meaning to the higher points.

Is it necessary to take a roller coaster ride to surmount a break-up? Certainly not! However, from my experience, it can be an uplifting thrill to refresh oneself. On the other hand, if you can be strong enough to get over a break-up without any frightening challenges like roller coasters and horror houses, I definitely give you a thumbs-up!

7. Knowledge, My Savior

What supported me to overcome the painful days was knowledge. It supplied my mind with nutrition while I was immersed in the emptiness, and illuminated the way for me while I was drowning in the darkness. Knowledge was my savior during this break-up.

To battle my frustration from the emotional crisis, I started to seek help from relationship professionals. I watched online videos created by inspirational speakers and relationship coaches and read relationship advice books. In addition, I researched studies about how the human brain functions, as well as theories of psychology.

By digesting more information and gaining knowledge, my brain was nurtured, my eyes were brightened, and my body was fueled with energy.

I was enlightened by many authors and advisers, especially two social influencers: Jay Shetty and Matthew Hussey.

Jay Shetty

The first month following my break-up was the most challenging time for me. Luckily, Jay Shetty's video rescued me.

As I mentioned in Section 2 (Logic vs. Emotion), Mr. Shetty's video "If They Left You - WATCH THIS" gave me a clear explanation of the importance of letting go of someone who was wrong for me. In the video, while a bride and her groom-to-be are on their respective ways to their wedding, she calls him. At the end of the phone call, the groom says, "I'm sorry. I can't do this."

Then, Mr. Shetty explains in the video after showing the story: "Even at your best, you will never be right for the wrong person."

I cried after I watched that video, for that poor bride in the story, as well as for myself. That scenario was so sad, but it was a practical illustration for me. I had done my best in this withered relationship, or perhaps I could have done a bit better. Yet, I understood it was not my fault. Even if I had done better, I still would not have been good enough because I was wrong for him and he was wrong for me.

The solution was simple: let go and move on.

Matthew Hussey

After initially searching "break up" on the social network, I started receiving automatically suggested videos related to break-ups. That was how I found Matthew Hussey, a relationship coach on social media who provides audiences with his advice on romantic relationships.

In many of Mr. Hussey's videos, he explains a specific point of view through different scenarios. By watching his videos, I learned not only about dating skills, but, more importantly, the intricate mysteries of relationships, such as redressing miscommunication, implications of language, the art of intimacy, and the virtue of respect. I considered his videos to be useful psychological references.

Having studied more about dating and relationships, my heart felt soothed. Some of those theories about romantic relationships can also be applied to other types of relationships, such as those with family members, friends, colleagues, and business partners.

As I discuss in Section 40 (Psychology and Me) of Chapter IX (Set Free), I started reading about psychology to learn more about the scientific study of the mind and behavior, useful elements to improve my EQ.

Having strengthened myself with a broadened vision, I moved forward with courage and confidence.

8.   Cut It Off If It Is Rotten

Applying the analogy of chopping off one's rotten toe in order to save one's foot, this break-up made me feel like I had to cut off my ex-relationship to save my sanity and create a chance for a peaceful life. Just as losing my toe would be sore but necessary for the sake of the rest of my foot, this figurative amputation of my putrid relationship would also be painful but necessary.

To symbolize the discarding of my former relationship, I cut my hair short.

Let the past go.

Nothing could stop me from surviving this break-up!

9.   Sunk Cost

I want to share my views about a failed relationship from an economic angle to explain the situation rationally.

As an Information System & Management major in college, I was fascinated by my Financial Management course, in which I learned about **sunk cost**—a useful term in both financial management and daily life. When my professor first introduced the concept of sunk cost to us, he started the lecture with the following story:

"I have a friend who was going through a tough time after his girlfriend suggested they break up. My friend said to me, 'I spent more than thirty thousand dollars on our trip to Europe not long ago. Now she is breaking up with me. If she leaves me, all the time and money I spent on her will have been for nothing.' Then I told him, 'The expenditure of your trip is a sunk cost. That expenditure will not be refunded, nor stop her from breaking up with you. The money you paid for her will not create any future value to this broken relationship, so forget about the money you have already spent and move on!'"

Put simply, a sunk cost is, according to Investopedia, a well-known internet source of financial content, "an expense that has already been incurred and thus cannot be recovered." I comprehend it as the cumulative money and effort I put into the past that will not physically contribute to any part of the future. This is reality that I have no choice but to accept.

Let's look at a break-up from material and mental standpoints. Objectively, the money, time, and effort spent on an unsuccessful past relationship are sunk costs. Thus, one should just leave the perished relationship behind and move on. Yet, virtually all past experiences constitute the footsteps in a person's lifetime journey, and every step brings him/her wisdom. One may take it as a lesson that will be helpful for the rest of his/her life. From an optimistic point of view, I always consider the time, effort, and money I put into something important as the educational fee I have paid for that experience, whether it turns out to be feasible or not.

Please do not be discouraged—sunk costs occur very often in daily life, so it is likely that you have already dealt with them. Life is meant to be a sum of all sorts of experiences and feelings, from bitterness to happiness, from naivete to maturity.

10. **Turning Point in a Dark Cycle**

Bad things come in cycles, just as good things do.

Like the butterfly effect, bad things happened to me one after the next starting from my break-up: we broke up; I was sad; I became sleep-deprived; I lost my appetite; I got sick; some of my business deals were rejected; my mother criticized my career choice; when my credit card bill arrived, I did not have enough money to pay it off, leaving me with no choice but to apply for payment installments despite being clueless about my future income.

I was sick and tired of my stressful situation, brooding on how awful my life had suddenly become.

It was one of the few terrible times in my life. I was in a bad state mentally, physically, and financially. I kept asking myself one question: how can I get over this dark time?

If you have ever been in a dark cycle, you may understand how demoralizing it can be—important aspects of your life are at their lowest points.

How can one break out of a dark cycle? It is very hard to turn the whole situation around right away. If one is trying to fix the entire predicament instantly, nothing is likely to happen, which can be very frustrating. From my experience of rebooting my life after the break-up, I have learned that the easiest way is to first figure out the turning point.

Where does my dark cycle come from? Good question!

What is the turning point of the whole situation? Good question!

Take some time to reflect on these two questions for yourself.

As with the butterfly effect, a favorable outcome may stem

from a small positive output.

So, let me come up with a small goal that I am able to achieve today:

Can I get rich and enjoy a fancy lifestyle immediately? Not very likely.

Can I obtain a degree and improve my life with a new career quickly? Not very likely.

Can I get over this break-up overnight? To be honest with myself, no.

The easiest thing I can do is recharge myself, just like I charge my phone. Even if I cannot fill myself up to 100%, 80% is pretty good, 60% is OK, and 30% is better than nothing.

Just make something happen today, OK?

I constantly told myself:

The first turning point is my ENERGY.

Without energy, I could not recover from my sickness, so the first step was to recharge my body's battery. My goal was to be a generator that could produce energy. The primary task was to replenish my inner force so that I could have the power to turn myself into that generator.

During my dark days, when I was suffering from the emotional breakdown and the flu that came with it, feeling physically and mentally collapsed, I told myself, "Everything is dreadful now, and I cannot change anything at the moment anyway. So, imagine the world is frozen today and make a getaway."

Therefore, for a long weekend after I contracted the flu, I did not work on anything. I got out of bed and ate, and then lay back in bed with music on. I emptied my mind and sang along to whatever was playing. Then, I went out into the street. I wandered around and tried to stop thinking. I did everything slowly. Even though I could not sleep much under the impact of the heartache, I stayed in bed for ten hours a day to let my body recuperate.

After this three-day energy replenishment, I began to recover from the flu. I started to feel some strength. I knew that this was a good turning point.

After regaining some energy, the second step was to rectify my attitude.

I can be down for a while, but not forever! I have to believe that a rainbow will present itself after the storm.

Two weeks later, I recovered from the sickness. Having survived the flu with the added sadness, I made up my mind to convert my melancholy mood into momentum for bettering myself. I went out jogging in the morning regularly. I planned my days ahead of time. I focused on only one business deal each day so that I could concentrate. Almost every day, I made time to write lyrics for my songs and paragraphs for this book. I had an imaginary funeral for myself to let go of the past. I cut my hair short to refresh my look. Slowly, over the course of two months, I got my health and my mood back on track. I gradually took control of my days again. Instead of frustration and depression, I felt delighted about the life I had earned, despite the fact that my heart was still silently bleeding.

Following the initial turning point, I kept up my exercise routine. I jogged almost every day, even for just twenty minutes on my busy days. I also went to cardio class at least twice a week. Step by step, I made progress in my business deals. I spent time hanging out with family and friends once a week to keep myself socialized. I kept working on this book to turn my sorrow into something memorable.

Starting from that carefree weekend, and over the following six months, I gradually got my life back on the right track. I knew that one day, luck would open the door for me again.

To turn around an unfavorable situation, your effort should be focused on every crucial aspect—your health, attitude, and career. Patience and stamina must be your companions.

One's dream cannot be accomplished overnight. If you aim to create a huge fire, start by making a spark.

*Have you ever thought about restarting your life?

Chapter III   Revealing My Dark Side

11.   The Ghost Inside Me

I wonder: does everyone have a hidden dark side? I guess I have one under my skin.

My dark side is like a ghost. I do not always know where she is or when she will come out. My dark side is a drive within me that urges me to surpass my old self.

Break-ups are never easy. Admit it.

In those heartbroken days, I felt lost, but I acknowledged the fact that he and I were done.

Going through an inexplicable pain, I realized that the way to help myself heal would be to let my dark side out, and then let it go.

Following my break-up, the presence of my ex in my mind haunted me constantly. I tried to distract myself from thinking of him, but my efforts were in vain. I was thoroughly tired of being enslaved by the emotional distress, so I finally gave in and admitted to myself that he and I were history. One last time, on a quiet night, I played out our entire story in my head. Lying in bed, I thought about how he had treated me from the beginning and how many times he had disappointed me. I counted from one instance to another. My tears flowed down my face while the scenes and his hurtful words replayed in my mind. It felt like my heart was being torn apart and my stomach was being pulled out of my body by a bloodthirsty beast.

Anger, hatred, resentment, disgust ... all these dark feelings rushed into my chest. I had never felt so awful before. It was like a black hole had sucked out all my blood and breath, and then left my dried-out body on the ground.

I really loathed this feeling, yet I had no way to expel it. The emotion affected me like a magnet—when I tried to push it away, it just drew more strength out of me. I was exhausted, hopeless, and desperate.

Then, I looked at myself in the mirror, feeling sorry for my crying face. My dark side came out.

She told me:

You are better off without him.

Be a successful person.

Prove it!

Then she left.

I made a vow to myself: **"Reach your best self!"**

At that moment, I committed myself to advancing my life:

From now on, I will set a balanced schedule for my work, fitness, relaxation, and sleep. I have to follow a healthy routine to build up a sturdy body and soul. There is no excuse for being lazy. I will wipe off my sad face, remedy my sleepless nights, rebuild my spirit, and banish my loneliness. I have to turn myself into a combination of different types of goodness.

My life goals then became clear: make money, strengthen my body, walk out with grace, and always stay youthful.

My honesty told me that my jealousy was the demon at my back, spurring me to strive.

I wished this would come true:

One day when we are older, if we happen to encounter each other again, he will be surprised that I look just as hot as I did in our youth. He will feel bad while I feel good.

I wanted revenge.

I told myself:

The best revenge I can take is to live a better life for myself!

I wondered:

The power of being in love versus the power of breaking up: which is stronger?

This emotional lash reminds me of the movie *Black Swan*. When the evil inside you appears, you may become capable of doing something beyond your awareness. Your dark side whips you forward, driving you to excel. Though you may be rough on yourself throughout the process of your transformation (setting higher expectations for yourself, working extra hard to achieve your goals, and developing stronger willpower), you will, thanks to this evil, reach the most epic version of yourself!

I had an even darker thought: I did not want to be an angel anymore. I hoped that when he was sleeping with someone else, he would still be thinking about me. That was how the darkness in my spirit inspired me to write the song "Call My Name":

Call My Name

Baby, when you feel like kissing someone
Please call my name
When you feel like touching someone
Please call my name
Whenever you are, wherever you go
Please call my name

Baby, when you are sleeping with someone
Please call my name
When you are feeling high with someone
Please call my name
Whenever you are, wherever you go
Please call my name

Baby, where are you?
How have you been these days?
Why don't you give me a call?
How is your day when you are away?

Remember the time we hung out
You said I was silly like a child
I told you how I got obsessed with you
You told me that I was not the only one

I saw you in my dream last night
Your skin was glowing in the light
Just like the last time you had a glass of whiskey
Your favorite drink when you were playing with me

I was wearing the lipstick you like
Walking into a bar where you gave me a surprise
I felt like I saw your shadow at the table
Where you called my name with a halo

Remember the scent on my neck?
Why are you still keeping my scarf in your closet?

Now I'm no longer an angel
You turned me into a devil
I'm up to another level
I'm ready to let go

12. Me as an Actor

This was me while under the black cloud of my break-up: I really did not want to smile. I did not even have the strength to summon a happy face. Nothing could lift my spirits.

I seemed active in front of people: smiling, talking, telling jokes, being passionate ... but I was just acting in front of everyone.

When I was alone, I could drop my mask and be myself. I was numb. I stayed in a daze. I shed tears. I gazed at my reflection in the mirror and wondered who that was staring back at me.

Perhaps I desired too much; I set my goals too high; I was pushing myself too hard ... I just had to admit that things had not turned out the way I wanted.

Who has not experienced a moment of feeling down? We can be faced with failures in relationships, work, and study—efforts in vain; being misunderstood, mistreated, betrayed—something unfair. Things are unpredictable. Life is an unscripted play.

To be honest with myself, I did not feel all right. In fact, I felt miserable. I needed a moment to express my moodiness, a break from acting OK in front of everyone.

*Are you truthful with yourself?

----

13. Selfishness: The Animal Instinct

Nowadays, this world is so competitive—if I am just good, I am not good enough! I have to be great to stand a chance to shine. I have to be *one in a million* to stand out. So, I have to fight: fight for the best me; fight against the worst me. Competing against others in order to survive is a rule of nature.

The primal animal instinct is to survive by feeding and reproducing—the key to which I believe is selfishness. By nature, animals do not perform acts of charity. An animal's top priority is itself and its offspring. However, over time, human beings have developed intelligence, emotion, integrity, and empathy. We take other people and the environment into consideration to become stronger in the form of community. That is why groups of people came together to establish different countries. Thus, one's selfishness is governed by his/her wisdom.

Nevertheless, selfishness is embedded in our bones. I understand that there is no point in blaming anyone for being selfish. That is why I have never blamed my ex for the break-up. Despite the fact that selfishness is an inborn survival tactic, a bright person still knows how to control his/her instinctive selfishness. If one is selfish without proper control, he/she is just not that wise.

In a romantic relationship, if two people cannot work things out, blaming one party for being selfish is useless. A better way out is to acknowledge that fact and let it go.

Regardless of selfishness being an innate quality within everyone, what I can do is make sure that my selfishness does not harm anyone else.

Maybe this is so-called "karma" or the idea that "what goes around comes around." I broke up with my first boyfriend fifteen years ago because I put myself first and left him. That break-up gave him a hard time. Now, it was my turn to get hurt by my loved one. This world is fair somehow.

If my first boyfriend could survive our break-up fifteen years ago, I should be able to find my way to survive this break-up too.

Selfishness, the underlying cause of a break-up, is driven by one's instincts. After letting go of a failed relationship, love yourself and care for your life—it is not sinful to be selfish this way.

14. The Ugly Side of Being Human

Selfishness is one of our animal instincts because we need to survive. Selfishness is also the origin of human beings' bad qualities, like laziness, greed, aggressiveness, and jealousy.

I felt that I had been exploited in this unsuccessful relationship. It was unpleasant to discover the ugly side of a person who had been once so close to me.

Thus, I wanted to be wiser. I desired to figure out people's ugly sides. People may put on a mask; people may smile when they do not mean it; people may say something while thinking the opposite; people may pretend to care about something when they actually do not.

I did not want to be mean or offensive. I just wanted to be a survivor in this world. I did not want to hurt anyone, and I did not want to get hurt by others. I just wanted to be a good person while keeping myself protected.

Now, in this competitive world, resources are decreasing, but people's desires are growing. Most of us strive to make a superior living. To become a capable person in this fierce contest, I should learn to see through people's shells and figure out what is inside them, while at the same time being clever enough to keep myself guarded. Behind a person's smiling face, there might be demand and greed.

To be a strong survivor in this world, where some people are inclined to exploit me for their own benefit and a lot of people compete with me, I have realized that I need to deploy my secret weapons:

- My talent: the greatest advantage that lies within me
- My willpower: the foundation of all my other qualities
- My resilience: the capability of self-healing after setbacks

In addition, my insight strengthens my competence. Life is a show and all participants are actors in it. A good mind reader may be able to perform better than the rest.

Everyone is a player in the game. If I do not want to be a loser, I need to be smart and a little bit sophisticated.

I am not trying to be villainous, but just to survive.

Human beings are advanced creatures. Beyond our basic animal instincts, we have developed wisdom and affection. People care not only about *themselves*, but also *their offspring*, *their partners*, and *their groups* because we will be much stronger as a team than as lone survivors.

I was born selfish by nature, but I am wise enough to care about people and things around me in order to be more powerful. I feel love in addition to the urge to survive. Life is at its most spectacular when there are beautiful living creatures around me. Humans also enjoy respect, appreciation, praise, and love. These are other forms of treasure.

*What are your thoughts on selfishness?

----

15. Defending Myself on an Emotional Level

From this break-up, I learned something important that I had not paid enough attention to before: how to defend myself on an emotional level.

I try to be nice to people, but some people have not always been nice to me in the same way. I want to be prepared for this so that I will not be surprised or even hurt.

Some unpleasant experiences from my withered relationship taught me a lesson. Besides using me for his own benefit, I recalled how my ex hurt my feelings on purpose again and again to drive the break-up.

Based on my own experiences, if someone intentionally hurt my feelings, either of the following could be the case:

1) he/she wanted to provoke an argument, leaving me no choice but to let go, or

2) he/she attempted to irritate me as a form of retaliation. If I got upset by his/her intended agitation, he/she would achieve his/her goal. That meant I gave him/her what he/she wanted—he/she won.

The best way to defend myself on an emotional level is to refrain from being irritated, no matter how much someone antagonizes me.

Easier said than done. It really requires an unbreakable heart to take on a compelling emotional challenge.

If someone tries to hurt my feelings again, I will tell myself, "I am not going to lose to that person! Despite everything he/she has done or said to me, my mind cannot be bothered. I should care less about something irrelevant. I live my life the way I want, not in someone else's shadow."

Whether or not I take on someone's unfriendly challenge, I should defend myself on an emotional level, and know when and how to walk away.

*Are you capable of defending yourself emotionally?

----

16. Revenge: How Much Would Be Enough?

After going through a break-up or finding out that you have been cheated on, it is natural to feel angry deep inside. I have been there. If you want revenge, I do not blame you. Well, imagining smart revenge may comfort you during a horrible heartbreak. Here are some plots I have crafted to go about it:

*Warning: The following are my humorous ideas for revenge strategies, offered just to make you laugh.

The concept is:

As I grow better and stronger, I will be entertained by watching him rot.

Why? Since he gave up on me, I would not mind watching him go down.

The greatest ability I gained from going through my break-up was letting my imagination run wild. The highest level is:

NO SHAME!

Three months after the break-up, he began texting me again, almost once a month. I cried every time I saw his text messages, as I could not suppress the flood of my emotions—my mixed feelings resurfaced. Later, after surviving my agony, I became better at controlling my emotions, so I started to play tricks on him as revenge.

In this game of words, the presentation can be flexible and creative in its style—the general idea is to immerse him in an ocean of boiling emotions.

I believed that acting with complete fearlessness in my responses would reflect that I was finally strong enough to ride the tide of the heartache.

Let me show you a few examples of how to be a heartless person and play him back (only for your amusement, as this content may be too spicy):

A. If he asks you, "Where do you live now?" or "How is your day going?":

If you respond:	
I am fine. It's not your business anymore.	*I'm doing very well. Thanks! Now, I'm living a few blocks away from the neighborhood where we lived when we were together.* (Imagine your eyes rolling while replying with these teasing words.)
—Wrong! If you say this, you sound like a winner, but you are going to terminate his fantasy about you. This is not revenge.	—Good job! Now you are going to arouse him by making him recall the good old days.

B. If he suggests catching up with a coffee:

If you respond:	
I don't think it's going to happen.	*Sounds fabulous, but I guess your new girlfriend would not allow that, unfortunately.*
—Wrong! If you say this, you will stop his interest in you. This is not revenge.	—Good job! Now the blame is on someone else. It may cause a fight between him and his new girlfriend if he is foolish enough to ask her for permission to see you.

C. If he sends you a holiday greeting:

If you respond:	
No reply, or *I do not need your greetings anymore.*	*Hearing from you is really unexpected but sweet. It was probably sent by mistake. Anyway, Happy Halloween!*
—Wrong! If you say this, you will only make yourself look impolite and rude. This is not revenge.	—Good job! Now you sound so pleasant and a bit intriguing. You can speak politely without really meaning it. Nothing beats a passive-aggressive response! Congratulations!

D. If he asks you if you are dating another man:

If you respond:	
Oh, yes. I have found a wonderful man who makes me truly happy!	*I'm not going to love anyone else like I loved you. You always hold a special position in my heart.*
—Wrong! This will only upset him for a short time. By saying this, you will let him realize his problems, improve himself, and then move on. He will treat the next woman better. This is not revenge.	—Good job! You can make him fly in the sky! He will think about you all the time. He will think that you are better than any other woman. He will suffer from missing you for a long time.

E. If he texts you that he misses you:

If you respond:	
That's not necessary.	*That's nice of you. Same here.*
—Wrong! If you say this, there is no chance to take revenge.	—Good job! You can start playing him back now! This response is like a sugar-coated poison pill. He will keep missing you.

F. Then, if he asks to see you:

If you respond:	
That's not likely to happen.	*That would be nice, but I understand that you're not allowed to.*
—Wrong! If you say this, there is no chance to take revenge!	—Good job! Now the blame is on someone else. You will not see him anyway, so why not talk some nonsense and let him feel disappointed?

G. If he insists that he misses you and wants to see you:

If you respond:	
OK, if you really want to.	*Missing is a kind of beauty.*
—Wrong! Are you kidding? He is probably sleeping with other women now. What will you get out of meeting up with him? Are you willing to give him what he wants? You will just be selling yourself out. Do not be fooled again!	—Good job! Let him keep missing you. Do him a favor: let him experience what you have been through.

H. If he says that he still loves you:

If you respond:	
It is over.	*Same here. I'll always love you like before. Whatever makes you happy, I'll be happy for you. I wish you all the best.*
—Wrong! Now, he is heartbroken, but that is not enough!	—Good job! Now you have learned to say what you do NOT mean. High EQ! High five! Yay! Having left you will be his biggest regret for the rest of his life. That is the best punishment for him. Let him enjoy the bitterness.

Now, you probably get my idea: words are cheap, but their impact can be as powerful as a sword. Punching him in the face will only hurt him for a while, and that is NOT ENOUGH! Causing him to regret will hurt him long-term—this is taking revenge!

Let me tell you how brazen I was one day, seven months after the break-up. I texted him:

"Hi, happy holidays! I recently heard the song 'Like I'm Gonna Lose You,' and it brought back those feelings of loss. If I had known that last January was going to be our last time together, I would have swallowed all the sadness to leave us with better memories, instead of dramas. I hope that you remember the good about me, not the bad. Anyway, I lost you, but I found myself. I am getting back to my normal life. I wish you all the best."

He replied that he remembered only the good about me and was thinking about me positively.

These two people seem to be on such good terms, but do you think my words were genuine? It took a high EQ to express what I wrote in the message. Shameless! Well, he, having no compassion for me, probably forgot about what a hard time he had put me through. I had achieved my goal through this conversation: he was thinking about me positively. An even better result would have been making him miss treating me like his obedient puppy or submissive maid.

Now, if he compared other women with me in terms of kindness, no one else would win against me. He might blame other women for being demanding or difficult. He had been spoiled by my generous nature. I did not have to educate him, but other women would. If I told him point-blank what his problems were, he would, initially, dislike me, because people prefer hearing compliments to receiving criticism (once he complained that my suggestion that he should use protection if he had physical interaction with others sounded like his mother's). Secondly, he would become aware of his problems, improve himself, and treat other women better. I did not want to point out his weaknesses to help him grow up, because since he dumped me, I no longer had to care what would happen to him, and I was not under such an obligation.

OK. This is me, a cunning woman. See what he turned me into?

Chill out! I understand that fantasizing about revenge reveals that I am not fully over the break-up.

I am sure that, once I am truly over him, I will be able to simply enjoy my own life without thinking about any of these schemes.

Will taking revenge really make you happy? Maybe, but just for a little while. **Please understand that revenge plots are only Band-Aids that temporarily cover the wound. They can only hold you over and conceal the pain while you are still enduring the heartbreak.** When you are completely healed by time and your strength, you will not have to be fake or sly. If you are generous and magnanimous enough to appreciate the past relationship or give your ex a second chance, why not do so? The best state in life is enjoying love and peace.

*Did my "revenge strategies" make you laugh?

Chapter IV   What Have I Done Wrong?

17. Unrealistic Expectations

I think the biggest mistake I made was having unrealistic expectations. I had a glimmer of hope that a miracle would occur, but that was merely my wishful thinking.

It was the loss of hope that submerged me in bitterness.

Unrealistic expectations in a romantic relationship are the origins of the downfall. This perished relationship made me feel much worse than my other failures did.

Even though I have always been a hardworking person, I have experienced a few major failures in my life. Eventually, however, I managed to move on from each of them. Those setbacks actually became accelerators that pushed me forward.

My first significant failure occurred when I was nineteen and was not accepted into my first-choice university. I successfully entered another university, also a prestigious school, but it was just not the one I desired most. At that time, it was the worst situation I had ever faced. For six years during high school, I studied diligently to prepare for university admission. This was my top priority at that age, and I aspired to enter my dream university to set a strong foundation for my future career.

Unfortunately, despite countless efforts in my schoolwork, I did not achieve my goal. For at least a year after I received my results from the annual Chinese National College Entrance Examination, I remained disappointed. I kept questioning myself about why I had not performed well enough. I wished I could go back in time to retake it.

However, I realized that I could still learn and study well at any university, as long as I put my heart into it. So, I persevered during my four years on campus, where I attended classes from morning till evening, and spent most of my time after class including weekends doing homework.

As a result of my diligence, I remained in the top ten to fifteen percent of my class according to the ranking by grade-point average (GPA). This remarkable academic performance rewarded me with two first-prize annual scholarships for the first two years, and one second-prize scholarship for the third year. By the end of my four-year college study, I graduated with two bachelor's degrees, one in Information System & Management (Electronic Commerce) and the other in English, which became an excellent foundation for my career.

Even though I had not studied at my top-choice university, seeing the accomplishments from my assiduity replaced my sadness with satisfaction. With proof of my outstanding performance at academics and my competent communication skills, I was able to compete with the rest of society and landed a promising job in auditing upon graduation. I have always been proud of every school I attended.

Another significant setback I encountered was not completing the Chinese licensing test to become a certified public accountant (CPA). Right after graduation, when I was twenty-three, I was employed by a world-renowned accounting firm, where one of my key objectives was to obtain CPA licensure. To achieve it, I had to pass six tests, each for a specific sector related to auditing.

Over the course of five years, I spent countless weekends and most of my annual leave (and even nonpaid leave) preparing for the tests instead of enjoying any relaxing vacation time or dating anyone. I devoted myself to the study and building my career. With a great number of hardworking days, I passed five out of six tests, but sadly I could not pass the test on Financial Management, even after multiple attempts. On three occasions, I was just a few points short of meeting the passing mark.

To this day, I still have not passed the test of this subject. This has been a huge pity. Due to this deficiency, I have not been able to become a licensed CPA. Years ago, as I changed my career from auditing to creative writing, I hit pause on attempting to retake the CPA exam. Not having passed this exam has been the biggest disappointment in my life by far. However, I understood that I should focus on my new career, writing, rather than hold onto something from my past.

From my experiences, I want to express that in terms of study and work, failures are not that scary. Based on my preparation for the test, I should have been able to estimate whether I would pass or not. I would then have been able to anticipate the results and be prepared for the worst scenario. In this case, even if I failed, I would have been able to replace my frustration with the incentive to improve myself and try again. I might have lost my shot, but I certainly would not have lost hope.

A failure in a romantic relationship, however, is much more destructive. When my lover left me, it seemed that nothing could replace him, as my attachment to him was rooted deep in my heart. Love is so powerful that it can beat my sanity black and blue. It is a sad truth that emotional involvement is incredibly profound.

In a romantic partnership, I should first ask myself: What do I want from him and what can he give me? I need to set realistic expectations to avoid getting seriously hurt. It may not entirely prevent me from being harmed, but it will at least keep the pain at a tolerable level.

18. I Do Not Have to Be OK All the Time

For the first two months after my break-up, I forgot how to smile. I had to make a great effort to act normal and pretend to be happy in front of people. I looked tired, worn, and much older. I had no choice but to admit to myself that I was not OK.

But guess what? I do not have to be OK all the time.

Disagreeable things happen in life: I tried and I failed; I lost something I valued; I missed out on opportunities. What can I do? I should be brave enough to acknowledge these unfortunate realities. If I am NOT OK today, just let me be.

One day, not long after the break-up, I was sitting on a bench alone in a small park next to a busy main street. Before, I had always been too busy to look at the cars and people passing by. This time, I sat there quietly, taking a moment to think about my position in this world. I wondered, "Why am I here? What am I doing here? This world seems to be unrelated to me. People have their plans and destinations, but I am stuck in the middle of my journey. When will I get over all this?" Warm tears were streaming down my face, chilled by the blowing wind. In front of this dynamic street, I sat in my emptiness, feeling isolated from the world.

I reached a brief moment of clarity. I trusted that many beautiful things would happen to me soon, so I consoled myself: "Take it easy. You don't have to be OK all the time."

Be true to yourself!

19. Does He Want Me or Not?

I tried to position myself as an outsider to review my past relationship from an unbiased angle:

If he wants to be with you, he will be able to accept your flaws, or at least suggest solutions, because love makes a person patient. If he does not, he will come up with different reasons as to why you two are not a good fit for each other.

Have you ever begged someone to come back to you? If so, I beg you to wake up!

So, what is the real reason he cannot continue to be with you? *"He's just **not** that into you."*—let me quote this famous expression from the book with the same title, written by Greg Behrendt and Liz Tuccillo.

If someone wants to be with you, he/she will propose plans to overcome any obstacles in the relationship, instead of voicing empty complaints.

Everyone has an ego. If someone is not proud to be with you, he/she may just store you in his/her secret life for pleasure once in a while. (Please do not be upset if I have offended you here. I have been treated this way. I can tell you how disrespected I felt when my ex treated me as a toy, a part of his collection. Where was my dignity? Where was my self-esteem?)

Now, time to wake up!

In reality, a person pursues certain qualities in his/her potential partner. If there are problems in my relationship, instead of blaming the other party, I should first think about what I can do to improve myself. The objective is to refine myself for myself, not only because I need to please a man.

20. The Balance

Not long after my break-up, I gave advice to a friend who was going through a complicated lawsuit. I reminded her, "The adjudication of this case will either be innocent or guilty. By law, there is no room for sympathy."

This also triggered me to think about what the rule of love is. Why is love so insane? By law, we see things in black and white, and there is no gray area. However, love is an intricate puzzle, and there is no "verdict." Why has our human nature evolved this way? Romance is a riddle. Without romance, it seems life would be simpler and easier. Why did evolution come to make simple things so complicated?

As a grown-up, I should be able to tell right from wrong, but in terms of love, I am such a fool.

How can I keep my feet firmly on the ground in the midst of such an emotional tornado?

It is a matter of balance.

Life is about finding balance: the point at which your emotional and physical states are at peace. If you find that balance, you feel happy. If you do not, you will probably encounter different kinds of turbulence. If the romantic relationship knocks you off your feet, you have to brace yourself to fight this disturbance.

Before the break-up, I always had doubts about our relationship because I felt uncomfortable very often. I knew that my ex and I were not a good match. Although I had noticed the signs and my concerns had been bothering me, I did not have the determination to cut it off.

At last, this feeble relationship fell apart. While confronting an emotional crisis, my life was totally out of balance. Although I seemed fine on the surface, busy working during weekdays and hanging out with friends on weekends, I was not genuinely enjoying my surroundings. I was still drowning in the gloom wherever I went. Life seemed invalid to me, even though people were bustling and events were happening all around me. Even exciting news that I heard at work did not truly boost my spirits. For months, I lived with a hollow body.

It took me a great deal of time and effort to gradually step out of the shadow and grasp the wheel of my life again.

This emotional collapse forced me into an acrobat's position. I did not want to fall, so I strove to find my mental balance by proactively trying different approaches to revive myself.

*Is your life in balance now?

----

21. <u>One Last Conversation</u>

My ex and I never had any insane fights, not even during our break-up.

Finally, two months after we ceased our relationship, I felt ready for one honest conversation to end our story. We met for the last time at a coffee shop to talk openly about the topics I had not had the courage to address previously. Before, I had been afraid of hearing his responses, but now, since we had already begun heading down different paths, I believed that I could finally speak my mind, acknowledge the truth, and conclude our relationship.

We spent an hour talking at an outdoor table in a quiet corner of a stylish coffee shop (it was funny that we happened to wear the same color that day—green). I teared up from the moment I started speaking. I was very calm but just kept weeping throughout the whole hour-long conversation. My face was flooded with tears.

In this final dialogue, I heard directly from him the answers to all those questions I had been wondering about. Although the truth was harsh, I accepted it bravely. At least I did not have to doubt anymore. I eventually came to a tremendous sense of relief. It was as though the clouds cleared up after a ruthless storm. This was the curtain call for the entire love story between us. It was indescribably painful, but it was a helpful approach that allowed me to surmount the past and move on.

So, the last conversation was our closing ceremony.

*What do you think is the best way to end a relationship?

Chapter V   Being Prepared for the Worst

22. What If I Run into My Ex After the Break-Up?

I hope that I do not encounter my ex again, not even after surviving the break-up. Why? Well, there is no point in refreshing my devastating memory of him and prompting a mental health disaster for myself once again, is there?

That was why soon after the break-up I moved out of the neighborhood where he resided and avoided going to the events that he usually attended. I knew that I would not be able to handle the pain of seeing him again.

Even if we were still around each other, I would have kept my distance from him. If we are no longer lovers, let's stay strangers.

In case you cannot cut the connection with your ex because of children, pets, properties, businesses, work, or other joint responsibilities, stay wise no matter what kind of challenge befalls you. **The general principle is: do not let emotions affect your judgment.** During your emotional or vulnerable time, avoid making critical decisions or carrying out significant tasks. You may take more time than usual to think about what to do and what NOT to do. Making a reckless move may take only a few minutes, but fixing the problem it causes may cost a lot of time and effort. Stay levelheaded and make sure you do things sagaciously. Talk to someone wise, or get help from reliable people or professionals if necessary. **Always remember that you are not alone.**

Although I am lucky that I can cut ties with my ex, I have to be prepared for the worst—what if I run into him, or even worse, him with his new girlfriend, accidentally at a public event? Am I going to freak out? Can I still preserve my composure? My reaction will reflect the stage of my recovery.

To protect myself emotionally, I have imagined the following scenarios of encountering my ex unexpectedly at an event (please only consider these ideas to cope with unwanted dramas as amusement):

A. If I see him, but he has not seen me, my reactions:

Not Over Him Yet	Over Him
▪ *Run away if this event is not important to me.* ▪ *Keep my distance from him and avoid letting him notice me if this event is very important to me and I cannot leave.*	*Ignore his presence and do whatever I have come here for. Avoid running into him. Even if he comes to say hello to me, simply respond with a "hello" back and quickly walk away.*
Why? It has taken me a great deal of effort to pull myself out of the spiral of sorrow. All I want is to kick him out of my life. Of course, I do not want anyone to disrupt my peaceful day.	Why? Having defeated the heartbreak is my victory. I am not willing to take a chance to get in touch with him to drag myself onto another emotional battlefield.

B. If he comes over to say hello and asks me, "How are you doing?" my reactions:

Not Over Him Yet	Over Him
▪ *If I am still in a terrible state, tell him: "I have been going through a tough time that you brought upon me, so please stay away from me."* Why? Just be honest with him and tell him that I am not OK. The biggest favor he can do me is to leave me alone. ▪ *If I am getting better at controlling my emotions and would like to spice it up, tell him: "I am doing well, but just missing something in my life."* Why? Since he put me into a tough emotional situation, I can serve him a witty response to activate his recollections of us.	*Briefly respond to him by saying: "Hi, what a coincidence. I'm doing very well. I believe you are, too. Excuse me, but I'm running to an appointment. Enjoy this event!" Then leave.* Why? Since there is nothing between us now, I do not want to chitchat with him to evoke any complicated emotions.

C. If he asks me for a lunch date after a short chat, my reactions:

Not Over Him Yet	Over Him
Refuse the offer by telling him: "It's very sweet of you, but I don't want you to see how emotional I am during the entire lunch. Next time."	*Refuse the offer by telling him: "Thank you, but since there is nothing between us now, I suggest you save your time for others."*
Why? I have come this far to heal myself. I absolutely do not want to hang out with him again and destroy my peaceful days. Yet, I can say something to arouse his interest in me, as a punishment for him.	Why? Since I am over him, I can simply treat him as a passerby. It will be smart to save my time.

What if I am faced with an even greater challenge—encountering him and his new girlfriend at a public event? My reactions could possibly be:

a. If I see him and his new girlfriend but they have not seen me:

Not Over Him Yet	Over Him
• *Run away if this event is not important to me.* • *Keep my distance from them and avoid letting them notice me if this event is extremely important to me and I must stay.* Why? An emotional challenge is no fun at all. I have to admit that I do not have an EQ high enough to deal with another mental breakdown as a result of seeing him and someone who took him away from me.	*Ignore their presence and do whatever I have come here for. Avoid running into them. Even if he or both of them come to say hello to me, simply respond with a "hello" back and quickly walk away.* Why? I should not be intimidated by my ex and his new girlfriend and I do not have to intentionally do anything to them. Also, there is no necessity of creating a friendly relationship with them. I am simply enjoying my own life.

b. Even worse, if this happens: they come over to say hello and he introduces his new girlfriend to me. After he mentions that I am his ex, she shows her pride. They ask me, "How are you doing?"

Not Over Him Yet	Over Him
Take a deep breath and do not panic! Even if fear, anger or hatred is burning inside me, stay calm! Although this is an incredible challenge, I must continue to act gracefully. I smile and tell them, "I am doing very well. Thank you. It has been a new era for me since your departure. I am really grateful for that. I'm sorry, but I have to run to a conference now. Hope you enjoy this event!"	*Say whatever I want, such as "Life has never been more fascinating! How about you?"*
Why? Although I do not have the courage to face up to them yet, I still uphold my dignity by showing my magnanimity.	Why? I am over it. I am free. I can speak my mind. If they want to throw me a challenge, I will bravely accept.

c. Worst-case scenario: if they invite me to their dinner party, or even their wedding!

Not Over Him Yet	Over Him
Show my excitement and respond by saying: "Thank you. I am going to bring my date. Let me check his schedule and get back to you." Why? Whether I really have a date or not, I can play it cool. Even if I do not have a date yet, I can simply make it up. Whether I am over him or not, **I am fearless now**!	

In general, I do not think that there would be any benefit from staying friends with my ex because I prefer to avoid any possibility of plunging into an emotional whirlpool again. After parting with my ex, I would like to restart my life with a clean slate.

This principle also links to the idea of being free-of-emotional-interference in doing business. I understand that mixing romance with work could be unwise, so I would avoid doing business with someone I had previously dated.

Just stay strangers with your ex unless this person is an indispensable part of your life. Let yourself heal first.

After you have entirely recovered from your break-up trauma, you can be liberated from the stress and feel free to do anything you want! Some people have no problem getting together with their exes to handle joint responsibilities, and some can even stay friends with their exes after recovery from the break-up wounds. When your EQ is high enough, you can live a life without fear or anxiety, so the key points are to get over the break-up efficiently and to fully develop your EQ. Hopefully, you will achieve these two goals after digesting the content in the rest of the chapters.

Chapter VI Quick Recipes for Break-Up Victims

23. Irrational vs. Rational Reactions to a Break-Up

Going through a break-up is no fun. It is like a perfect storm that is capable of destroying one's body, mind, and life. At one's most vulnerable moment, he/she may easily lose his/her sanity and react irrationally. A clear mind and strong willpower are crucial for dealing with emotional ups and downs.

Let's take a look at some examples of the differences between irrational and rational behaviors in response to a break-up. Note that heartbroken people may not be aware of the unfavorable or even harmful actions they take during an emotional breakdown:

	Irrational Reactions	**Rational Reactions**
Attitude	▪ Feeling disappointed with this world, including oneself; ▪ Living one's life in gloom; ▪ Thinking less of oneself; and/or ▪ Becoming cynical about love.	▪ Loving oneself and one's life even more; and ▪ Appreciating everything that one has, especially one's time.
Self-consolation	▪ Indulging oneself in excessive food, such as a lot of desserts and snacks; and/or ▪ Spending money lavishly to numb oneself.	▪ Taking care of one's health by maintaining a healthy diet and exercise routine; and ▪ Further developing one's talent to fully deploy one's potential.

	Irrational Reactions	Rational Reactions
Distraction	▪ Becoming unsociable and staying home for unproductive pastimes such as watching TV and playing games long hours; ▪ Getting drunk to hide from reality; and/or ▪ Jumping into speed dating recklessly to use a rebound as an anesthetic.	▪ Going out to meet new people and participating in meaningful activities; and ▪ Embracing one's new life with energy and conviction.
Temper Release	Venting one's anger by destroying his/her belongings: tearing things apart, breaking glass, damaging furniture, or burning the gifts from his/her ex.	Turning one's anger into power through physical exercise to breathe fresh air, sweat, and build a fitter body!
Revenge	Blaming one's ex and speaking derogatorily about that person.	Living a better life for oneself gracefully. Reaching one's best self!

Attitude determines the outcome. If a dreadful break-up happens, stay strong, no matter what! Think twice before taking impetuous actions. A heartbroken person does not deserve any undesirable consequences that arise as a result of a vanished relationship. **Be savvy and turn the challenge into an opportunity to transform yourself, just like the metamorphosis of a caterpillar into a butterfly!**

*Your thoughts:

----

24. Instant Steps to Recover from a Break-Up

Based on my arduous experience, here are ten quick healing recipes to cope with the challenge of going through a break-up:

1. **Cry in front of a mirror.** Think about all those bad moments throughout the relationship. Look at yourself. Believe what you see. Accept it (the hardest part is acceptance, but this is the breakthrough). Remember how awful you look at this moment. Never let anyone or anything break you again!

2. **Go out to meet new people and breathe fresh air.** Say "hello" to new faces. You will realize that there are many capable people out there and you have so much more to learn from them.

3. **Go out to do physical exercise and sweat!** Group activities, such as fitness and dance classes, can be helpful and fun. After crying in bed, go to the gym and perspire! Let the pain be your motivation! Let the sweat wash away your sorrow!

4. **Go on an adventurous trip to a new place.** It can be a new country, a new city, or a new area in your neighborhood that you have never been to before. Seeing something different can give you a fresh, new perspective. You will realize how much variety this world has to offer. Heartbreak is just a minor matter, and it does not deserve your precious time. Do not stay in the place where your old memories were made. Create new memories! Do not tie yourself to one tree, or you will miss out on the whole forest. Allow the new views of the world to amaze and astonish you!

5. **Receive compliments.** Simply talk to people and let them compliment you on your qualities, so that you discover more reasons to appreciate yourself. Just be mindful—do not go to

any unsafe place in search of a rebound. Do not put yourself at risk just because of heartbreak. Stay sober!

6. **Explore your artistic side.** Do something that kindles your imagination and creativity. Do some small yet satisfying activities such as singing, dancing, cooking, writing, painting, and crafting. My preference was writing because I felt that transforming my pain into productivity was a form of art. Many artists have developed their talents and produced amazing songs, poems, and other types of artwork after harsh break-ups. Gain something after you lose something.

7. **Confide your feelings in trustworthy friends (but not mutual friends, to avoid embarrassment).** Select your wise friends who can give sensible advice as outsiders and do not blame or judge. People who are rational may also give you insightful ideas that can bring out the best in you. Talk to professionals if necessary. They are able to analyze a situation objectively and give you an unbiased point of view.

8. **Hang out with friends who are in healthy relationships, too.** People in stable relationships may better know how to maintain a good relationship and solve relationship problems. They may also have had unsuccessful relationships in the past and then moved on. They are likely to give you the confidence to believe in love again.

9. **Watch videos by relationship advisors and inspirational speakers.** Here are some coaches on the Internet whose videos have been helpful for me: Jay Shetty, Matthew Hussey, and Dhar Mann. Although the opinions and scenarios they explain may not be exactly relatable for everyone, their perspectives can be enlightening and help you expand your views on tackling relationship issues.

10. **Drink enough water!** First of all, you may have shed a lot of tears, so prevent yourself from getting dehydrated. As you know, water is one of the most important resources for your body. Emotional troubles can disturb your daily life and cause health issues. A strong body is the foundation for defeating emotional problems.

In my own experience, an extreme way to console myself was to create a fictional scenario in my mind that our break-up had actually rescued me, as mentioned in Section 5 (A Little Imaginary Funeral for Myself). This is because a person tends to feel relieved and thankful if he/she believes that he/she has dodged a misfortune.

During my saddest time, when I felt the most vulnerable, I repeated this hypothetical notion in my mind over and over again to comfort myself: "Imagine: if this break-up had not happened, I could be dying from a disease or an accident caused by this unhealthy relationship. That could have been the biggest disaster for me. My future self has come back to the present to allow this break-up in order to save me. I have successfully escaped a tragedy!" This imaginary scenario was like a bucket of ice for my spirit, numbing me from sorrow. To look at things on the bright side, losing him was a GAIN, definitely not a loss. I repeated this to myself thousands of times and finally came to believe it. I trusted that after passing through this gloomy period, there would be a dazzling landscape on the horizon.

In the meantime, be mindful that there are situations to **avoid** if you have determined to let go of a relationship after careful consideration:

- Mentioning your break-up to the mutual friends you and your ex share until you are over the critical stage of the emotional crisis.

   In my own experience, the scariest question I received from our mutual friends was: "What happened between you two?" This always turned my day into a nightmare. It was like rubbing salt into my wound. Unquestionably, I would never want to hear my friends say, "I told you he was the wrong choice for you," "You can do much better," or "I can't believe he's such a fool." Besides, no one wants his/her relationship setback to be used as other people's gossip material, right? If they happen to ask about it, you can respond briefly by saying, "Yes, we moved on."

- Checking your ex's recent updates on social media.

   Do not be curious about what he/she is doing without you. People tend to show the glamorous sides of their lives on social media. Seeing your ex having a good time without you may cause you more anguish.

- Keeping in touch with your ex.

   If you have determined to break up with your ex, cut the connection off. Do not let his/her shadow drag you down.

What if your ex contacts you? There are three possible reasons why your ex tries to stay in touch with you:

a) He/She cannot let you go. This is an unfavorable pattern. This entanglement will make going through the break-up even harder.

b) He/She needs your help badly. If you are the only person in this world who can help him/her, then yes, please give support to someone who truly needs it.

c) He/She wants to continue to use you as before. In this case, think twice. If he/she can easily get help by hiring professionals, you can save your time and energy.

You can surely recover from a break-up in a graceful manner. Please remember to use **the power of suggestion**—affirm to yourself every day that this break-up is easy to overcome, not difficult. Confidence, optimism, and patience are all you need. In the end, you will be proud of yourself!

*What is your affirmation to yourself?

----

25. <u>Tips for Sleepless Nights</u>

Sleep is crucial for a person to regain energy and maintain good health. In terms of quality sleep, EQ plays a critical role by switching off the emotional alarm in a person's mind and allowing him/her to fall into deep slumber.

Were there times I did not perform perfectly at work? Yes, there were.

Were there times I did not achieve my goals during my studies? Yes, there were.

Were there times I missed out on chances in life? Yes, there were.

Disappointing things may happen unexpectedly at any time. It is important to be able to leave things behind and go to sleep with ease.

I have this problem: if something does not go right, it lingers in my mind and I cannot fall asleep. Even after I manage to get to sleep, I wake up in the middle of the night and continue to think about it. It is a bad pattern. The lack of sleep causes me fatigue and physical pain, and it takes me days to recover.

Sleeplessness was the most severe side effect of my break-up. In the first month, the most grievous time, my sleep patterns were chaotic. Many times, I worried that I was going to pass out while walking because I could not get more than five hours of sleep per night. I could feel pressure in my chest. I knew that my heart was already exhausted.

During those sleepless nights, my mixed feelings bothered me constantly. This break-up was inexplicably bitter for me, but I respected the fact that we had gone our separate ways. I never blamed him. I believed that as time went by, this emotional surge would eventually vanish.

Suffering from insomnia, I thought about buying sleeping pills countless times. However, as a person with pride, I held off every time at the pharmacy. I did not want to live a life dependent on medication because of my break-up, a minuscule event. If I had started taking pills to go to sleep, I might have fallen into addiction and would have relied on them forever. In that case, my life would have been trapped under the shadow of my ex, instead of remaining under my own control.

Why was my lousy break-up a big deal? It was just one small hurdle that I needed to jump over in the course of my life. My perseverance would certainly entitle me to get over this emotional hardship!

I must preserve my dignity when an emotional crisis challenges me!

Angela Lee Duckworth, a renowned psychologist, once gave a speech at a TED Talks event entitled, "What factor determines whether a student will succeed or fail?" She pointed out that it is GRIT.

Grit is the key factor that will lead you to success. I believe that surviving a break-up is an achievement, and grit plays the leading role here.

With a massive effort in reactivating my life, two months after my break-up, my sleep cycle gradually took a favorable turn. Although sometimes it was still not easy for me to fall asleep and my ex's presence in my dreams woke me up from time to time, the impact on my sleep reduced.

My break-up was a tough challenge, but I took it as an opportunity to foster my willpower. It was up to me to define my attitude toward the obstacles in my way.

Ten tips to cope with sleeplessness:

From my experience and the advice of therapists, here are some tips for battling sleeplessness (due to stress from emotional issues, work, study, etc.):

1. Do not try to force yourself to fall asleep quickly. The more your mind struggles, the more uneasy you become. Relax. The worst-case scenario is that you will see the sunrise and that is fine. If you are tired of visualizing yourself on a cozy beach, try fantasizing about something beautiful that has not happened yet to come up with new ideas for your life.

2. Eat something. Eating a small portion of food with carbohydrates and protein may make you feel sleepy as your stomach starts working.

3. Thinking too much? Write it down. You may lose a night of sleep anyway. Why not give yourself a nice paragraph as a gift?

4. Get up around your usual wake-up time instead of trying to compensate by getting up much later. If you have been suffering from an emotional challenge for a period of time, you may have endured some sleepless nights. Getting up late can temporarily recharge you, but it is not a long-term strategy. If you keep delaying your wake-up time for a long period of time, it may lead to a chaotic sleep schedule. Try to get into a routine of getting up around the same time.

5. Do a decent amount of exercise during the day to maintain physical and mental balance. Sweating makes you feel refreshed.

6. Drink enough water during the day to avoid health issues.

7. A short nap (around twenty minutes) during the day is a good way to recharge yourself. Be mindful that a long nap may disrupt your sleep pattern.

8. Use mobile applications for sleep assistance. Why not be open to modern technology? You may already know of some mobile apps that provide calming sounds to help you fall asleep. Also, there are sleep analysis applications that can detect your sleep cycles throughout the night. Although you do not need to rely on a tool to fall asleep, it can be helpful to discover more about your sleep.

9. Enjoy pure rest. You do not have to push yourself to extremes all the time. Take a day off if necessary.

10. Prepare for the night an hour in advance. For example, relax your body, reduce your speed, calm your mind, and turn down the lights. Enjoy a break from your daily work. Do not work on something complicated or stressful at night. Get ready to enter your sleep mode.

If you have an important activity the next day, get things ready a few days in advance so that you can take it easy the night before.

Regardless of knowing all the methods, sleeplessness may occur, but it does not have to be a big deal.

Many studies conducted on sleep and insomnia by professionals are available on the Internet, as well as in books and magazines. The knowledge about how to ensure the quality of sleep is worth digesting. You will quickly see the benefits after you improve your sleep, especially deep sleep, the stage in which your energy is restored and many parts of your body are regrown.

*In your sleepless nights, what did you do?

My break-up did not change my views on life,
but it navigated my way when I was lost.

Part Two   Understanding Life

Chapter VII What Do I Want After All?

26. What Do I Want from a Partner?

How can we find the right partner? Let's first think about our goals. If you have a feeling that the situation with the person you are currently dating does not seem to be consistent with your dating objectives, it is likely that an issue will eventually arise. Struggling in an unworkable relationship actually costs you unnecessary time and blocks you from finding someone who matches you.

I have conceptualized the following dating objectives, which logically pinpoint what one may look for in a partner. If you are considering ending an unhealthy relationship, the following scenarios, organized according to your economic situation, may enlighten you in identifying the reasons why this partner may not be a good match for you:

- If you are financially independent:

You would like to find someone to:	He/She is not the ideal one for you if:
Appreciate your qualities	He/She is very different from you and your qualities are not appealing to him/her.
Enjoy life with	He/She has a different lifestyle and does not share enough common interests with you.
Achieve a life goal with	His/Her mentality, values, and vision are different from yours.

- If you are financially dependent:

You would like to find someone to:	He/She is not the ideal one for you if:
Lead you in life so that you can have a shoulder to lean on	He/She is not a take-charge person.
Provide you with a secure life so that you do not need to struggle to earn a living	He/She can barely support himself/herself.
Provide you with a comfortable life, as you have a high lifestyle standard	He/She is very frugal with money.

Viewing my break-up from a logical point of view, I assured myself that dropping my former relationship was the optimal decision—I should not linger in the past; I must move on!

From my own dating experiences and my observation of both failed and successful relationships, here are some signs that reflect whether a couple is a bad or a good match:

A Bad Match	A Good Match
Speaking on different wavelengths	Being able to read each other's minds even without words
Becoming cynical about love life	Becoming more passionate about life
Becoming stressed	Becoming wiser
Aging faster	Looking vibrant
Finding everyday activities dull	Finding that time flies quickly
Feeling surrounded by obstacles	Feeling how lucky you both are
Creating issues for fights	Creating the worth of love

Apparently, being with an unsuitable partner can be like having chronic pain. Looking for the right mate is an endeavor that deserves your attention.

In fact, if you are in an uncomfortable relationship, you have probably already discerned the issues. You are just indecisive about breaking up because it is hard to let go.

Then, you might ask yourself, **what do I want from a relationship**? This is such a meaningful question. If I ever have my own wedding, I would like to give a speech like this:

You, Half of My World

The best state of a relationship is when both of us can enjoy each other's personality, beauty, and company. I am proud to have you, and you are proud to have me.

We do not feel it takes effort to be together. We are naturally comfortable with each other, while still retaining our own space and privacy. We share a lot of interests while keeping our differences. The bond between us is respect.

We have similar lifestyles and share the same values and vision. We are able to resolve difficulties together and turn "plain" days into "flavorful" times. There is nothing we cannot talk about. There are countless things we can converse about. Even when we do not speak, we can read each other's minds and feel each other's souls. Between us, a smile is guaranteed and tears only come from happiness. In short, we enjoy life together.

We are mature enough to take care of our own issues. Neither blame nor complaints exist between us as we contribute to our future willingly and equally. We bring out the best in each other and become stronger together. Not only do we know the definition of affection, but we also create the meaning of love.

We even extend our care to each other's families and friends because your world is also mine.

Over time, our love story will become a legend.

Since we are not immortal, we know that one day we will have to say goodbye to each other, but we will have no regrets when the day arrives where we must part.

Ask yourself: what does my ideal relationship look like? For me, it is a match in which our respective value coalesce into a meaningful whole.

*Have you ever thought about what you are looking for in a partner?

----

27. Envisioning My Future Mate

My break-up forced me to reboot my life proactively. I convinced myself that the disappearance of my ex was actually an opportunity for me to seek out the right partner. Envisioning the ideal companion comforted me during my most vulnerable time.

I recalled that once, years ago, a girlfriend and I came up with an idea of how to weigh a man's potential as a prospective serious partner, just like how an employer may assess an applicant at a job interview for a crucial position. This notion was created from the viewpoint of two self-sufficient women living in a highly competitive world. It may seem somewhat insensitive, but please be aware that this is only for your reference. I hope you will only take this in the spirit in which it is offered here.

Four Dimensions to logically consider the potential of a partner in terms of developing a long-term relationship:

1. Manners—the entry-ticket into a person's world

2. Wisdom—one's source of well-being

3. Personality—reflects the value of this person in this relationship

4. Participation in pursuing a career—contributes to the foundation of life

The scenarios include:

A. If someone scores 0 in any dimension, he/she is not an eligible candidate. Cases can be:

- Someone is smart and well-off, but is disrespectful to people.

- Someone is attractive but easily involves himself/herself in conflicts.

- Someone is wealthy but has unfavorable qualities (unfaithful, violent, rude, bad-tempered, etc.).

- Someone is supremely kind but refuses to learn and progress with respect to making a living.

B. A viable candidate can be:

Someone strong in at least one dimension, and acceptable in the rest.

C. An ideal candidate can be:

Someone very strong in at least one dimension and fairly good in the rest.

The framework above sounds sensible in a society with intense competition, doesn't it? Nonetheless, we should recognize that love is not always logical and sometimes can drive a sane person to lose his/her marbles.

From a heartbroken person's standpoint, setting reasonable expectations for a potential significant other can be a way of self-healing after ending a relationship with enormous pain. Having guidelines can provide one with the necessary confidence to move on. Just as a parent hopes that his/her child will date an upstanding person with good qualities, why not envision a promising prospect for yourself?

One Simple Way to Assess a Potential Relationship:

After dealing with all the challenges and afflictions from my past romantic adventures, I have devised a simple litmus test to consider whether or not to continue dating a specific person. All I have to do is ask myself the following question:

When I think of him, do I feel *stressed* or *pleased*?

Why? If my partner makes me feel stressed (a red flag), there must be something causing the tension, which might be one of the following:

- Financial burden: he can barely support himself, or he is in a financial crisis, etc., while I am not well off myself.

- Reputation: he is very social and surrounds himself with many women. I cannot stop myself from feeling anxious about him cheating on me. My friends and family have warned me about him being unfaithful. I worry that people feel sorry for me.

- Personality: he has a bad temper, and at times he is like a loose cannon, so I stay cautious when I am with him. I cannot be honest or relaxed when I communicate with him.

- Difference in interests: we like different things and do not share a lot of common interests. It takes substantial effort on my part to spend time with him.

- Background differences: regarding lifestyle, life goals, education, culture, values, and vision, I feel like he and I are from two different planets, living in two different worlds. It is unnatural when we are together and I cannot tell why that is exactly. He does not laugh at my jokes. He does not appreciate my value.

Of course, all relationships require effort in different ways and at different levels. But, if I feel *stressed* when I think of him, it may be a signal that I am going in the wrong direction with this person, and the more I move forward, the further I will be heading down a dangerous path. A serious relationship deserves my careful consideration.

*Your thoughts:

----

28. Risk Assessment for a Romantic Venture

Love is a complicated matter, and so is a romantic relationship. Sometimes I find them much more difficult than mathematical problems or economic theories.

Let's see how love interferes with one's life from the perspective of a person who is susceptible to heartbreak. What happens when I am in love, especially with the wrong person:

- No matter how much good news I hear, one hurtful sentence from him can entirely ruin my day; no matter how awful my day is, one sweet word from him can lift my spirits. Why is my day defined by him?

- I care about what he thinks much more than how I feel. I am not myself. I am totally lost.

- I always put him first and I cannot be fair to myself.

- When he brings me happiness, I feel stressed at the same time because I know I am getting more addicted.

- Those words he said haunt me day and night.

- I have wasted too much time expecting his reply.

- I cannot breathe because the feeling of missing him suffocates me.

- I know that what I am doing is wrong, but I cannot correct myself. The conflict in my mind never ceases.

- Jealousy drills my heart and makes it bleed.

- I am living in doubt and fear. Why am I anxious about losing him?

- Why do I always forgive him so easily, but I just cannot be lenient with myself?

- My emotion blocks my wisdom and rules my mind.

Falling in love is probably the most beautiful act in the world. Yet, it can be a risky act if your love flows like driving a race car full speed down the freeway.

Let's compare falling in love to beginning a new project. When providing financial services, a responsible service provider will first perform a risk assessment (or at least a risk analysis) before taking on a new client or starting a new project. I believe that this procedure should be implemented in a similar way when entering into a romantic relationship, although it may sound too stringent or ridiculous and dispel the sense of romance.

A short-term love affair can be wild, crazy, and insane. You may, however, consider a long-term relationship in a slightly different way because it is the real deal! **A serious love partnership can be deemed a business transaction, in which both parties are obligated to contribute equally. Fairness is the basis for balance and sustainability.**

So, how can we proceed with this risk assessment for a romantic venture?

Let's apply the concept of risk assessment in economics to the framework of evaluating the feasibility of a romantic relationship:

- Systematic risk (also known as inherent risk): technically, this means the uncertainty in the environment (including the market, related policies, interest rate, and inflation) that an entity cannot control.

    In terms of considering a candidate for a romantic relationship, the "environment" can be translated into: the surroundings in which this candidate grew up, the family in which this candidate was raised, the education this candidate received, and the culture in which this candidate lived.

- Business risk, which is under one's control, involves:

  - Operation: interpreted as one's personality, loyalty, lifestyle, hobbies, and passion;

  - Finance: interpreted as one's career path and style of spending; and

  - Reputation: interpreted as one's dating history. In other words, is this person known to be a player? In addition, people are very concerned about transmitted diseases these days (such as COVID-19). There have been news reports about people getting infected after love affairs, and then having infected their families.

I wonder if my ideas amuse you? I probably sound like a dull theorist, trying to apply rationality to a completely illogical subject: LOVE. Please understand that I came up with these analogies with the hope of enlightening you while you are "forecasting" the possibility of success in a relationship.

In business, risk assessment is the first critical step because it determines the viability of a deal. Regarding a love partnership, an honest appraisal is worthwhile (again, stay smart and savvy), unless the union is simply a furious romantic rendezvous.

*What are the factors you consider for a relationship?

----

29. Sex: "Don't Disrespect Me!"

I was really indecisive when I began writing this section, as I am a relatively conservative person, not one easily inclined to openly discuss sex. However, not mentioning sex when talking about a romantic relationship would seem incomplete. Hence, sex deserves a position in recognizing the intimacy between two people.

As a basic and natural instinct, sex is a beautiful matter. Yet, it can also be dangerous, toxic, and disastrous, because it creates a unique, subtle, mysterious, and profound bond between two lovers. It can be like an invisible demon that invades one's heart fiercely. It is able to drag one down into deep despair. Falling in love with a person when sex is involved is hazardous. Be very careful!

When an intimate relationship has fallen apart, sex plays the role of the villain. Sex makes the break-up more excruciating because the unique aspect it brought to the relationship is now lost. During my emotional storm, I tried replacing the disgust from my break-up with another awful feeling. Many times, I felt that watching something revolting (on social media and other sources) would cover the terrible feelings I endured when I thought about us involuntarily. It is the same concept as losing your appetite at the sight of someone else vomiting, isn't it? (Please forgive me for being so gross at this point.)

I read many tragic and horrific stories while I was depressed following the break-up. Sad things were my comrades, because knowing that there were more miserable occurrences out there made me realize that mine was not the worst.

Though my break-up caused me to perceive sex negatively, let's now look at sex in a normal context:

In a relationship, sex is a natural interaction between lovers. It is one of the two basic animal instincts—eating (survival) and mating (reproduction). Eating is not a shameful act, nor is sex.

I will try to explain it from my objective point of view: just like a mirror, sex can be a reflection of the closeness in a romantic relationship. If intimacy is gone, one critical aspect of the romantic bond will be weakened. After that, a couple is mainly bound by their material possessions, corporeal responsibilities (such as children, pets, finances, etc.), or companionship.

I have realized that the most important aspect of sex is engagement. It is not only the interaction of the body, but also of the mind and soul. For me, I would rather participate passionately, or not at all. The inclusion of mind and soul makes every inch of your body feel like it is burning. Meanwhile, your feelings flow freely. It is honest communication between two people. This is why, for some people, affection increases so much when physical interaction becomes involved; it touches you deeper than the surface of your skin, and you feel it inside your bones.

As such, sex deserves respect! I believe that everyone should be respectful of his/her sexual partner, whether in a serious relationship or a short-term fling. Some relatively conservative people, like me, may be subject to feeling more vulnerable after sexual intimacy has been established, because lovemaking can cause passion to grow intensely. Not everyone is able to easily separate their emotions from sex. Therefore, if someone is willing to have sex with you, that person is, to a certain extent, opening up his/her heart to you. So, please respect that! Sex is a sacred act.

On the other hand, how can sex be a demon? It can bring on not only mental pressure, but also physical issues. We have seen some appalling news reports about naive teenagers and young adults becoming infected with sexually transmitted diseases (STDs) through engaging in careless sexual activities. It is so unpleasant to hear about this. Actually, this is something so near to all of us in everyday life. How can we be reckless?!

Once I was chatting with my girlfriends about dating, while having drinks and desserts on a sunny afternoon. My friends were telling their stories of love affairs. I told them, "If I'm going to sleep with a man, I don't need him to take me to expensive restaurants or buy me luxury jewelry, but I will first ask him to show me his doctor's report to prove his clean physical status!" My friends all burst into peals of laughter, saying, "You're so practical. Yes, definitely necessary!" See, this is a wise person behaving in a realistic and prudent fashion. To partner with someone for romance, I require not only an honest personality, but also an STD-free body. I believe that not bringing any health issues to one's partner is RESPECT.

After major break-ups, people go through vulnerable times during which they tend to make mistakes more easily. Although I have always been quite an optimistic person, in the first three months following my break-up, nothing could genuinely make me laugh like before. I considered that if I went out to meet a new guy and slept with him, I would probably feel better, like taking a painkiller. However, I stopped myself every time I came up with this type of stupid idea! I learned this the hard way because my recent ex was actually a rebound partner after my previous ex, which had turned out to be a mistake.

Despite how much I was struggling to get through my break-up, I resolved that I would NOT destroy myself by sleeping with a random person. I would NOT live under my ex's shadow! I would be the master of my own feelings. I would only sleep with someone I sincerely liked and would **NOT do that as a rebound-emergency remedy**. After the break-up, in order to resume my normal life, I participated actively in public events and met several decent men with whom I became friends. I did not have any physical contact with any man until six months later, when I dated someone whose wonderful qualities indeed were attractive to me. No matter how ruinous my break-up was, I tried to make judicious decisions. Looking back, I am impressed by my grit.

Sex can be like a forbidden fruit. Think before tasting!

*Your thoughts:

----

30. The Experience of Dating a Desirable Man

Two months after my break-up, I started to meet new guys. I went out with several quality men, and they left me with great impressions. They gave me the hope that spring would eventually arrive after the long, cold winter.

When you meet admirable people, their value will fill you with faith in future dating.

Throughout my rebound dating experience, I encountered many humorous moments, one of which I would like to share here for your amusement:

Amy, a friend of mine, planned to introduce me to a charming guy because she wanted to help me move on. As Amy described, he was a good-looking, clean-cut, fit, and classy man, almost like a Ken doll—Mr. America. She excitedly informed me that he was interested in a date with me after she described me to him and showed him my pictures. This news heartened me during my emotional downturn. So, Amy helped us exchange phone numbers. After we texted each other briefly, we planned to meet up at a museum. However, he postponed our date several times with a common excuse: "Busy with work." I told Amy about this situation and then she discovered something that totally surprised us—she did an Internet search and found him active in online gay chatrooms! (I suppose you have just laughed out loud at this moment, right?)

Amy and I still giggle about it to this day. It was once a pretty bubble to me—my charming almost-date once made me believe that I still had my enchantment, even though the initial meeting never took place. Although this bubble did not last long, the good news to me was that I did not lose hope. I just needed more patience in my pursuit of the right mate.

In spite of the inevitable obstacles in the path of seeking love, I kept encouraging myself:

You WILL find someone who sees the grace in your soul.

With luck, I met some likable guys. From my perspective, here are the qualities that impressed me:

1. Manners:

Good manners do not necessarily mean him opening the door or offering to foot the bill after lunch (by the way, an independent woman should be able to pay her own bill or at least offer to pay her part!). More importantly, good manners should be presented as a friendly smile, consideration for others, graciousness, and respect.

2. Wisdom:

Wisdom is a combination of intelligence and life experience. He nourishes my brain and I become smarter after spending time with him.

3. Kindness:

A compassionate man truly touches my heart. He is a warm human being, not merely a cold-hearted survivor in this world. Being caring is a praiseworthy feature in a person.

4. Artistic talent:

This could be anything from writing, to painting, to crafting, to making music, to singing, to dancing, to cooking, etc. Creativity is what sets human beings above all other animals. Anyone can appreciate a man who is passionate about creative work.

One of the most helpful approaches to get over a break-up is to meet new people with the attributes you value. I once met a businessman who also played guitar and wrote music on the side, because he had the talent and enjoyed it. He told me that he composed songs when he was happy; I told him that I wrote when

I was sad. We listened to each other's music and spoke about writing. It was such a delightful time with someone who struck a chord with me.

I have been hoping to find a man who is a reflection of myself. Here is another example: six months after my break-up, I started seeing a longtime friend of mine. He and I got along very well. We enjoyed many meaningful conversations. The time we spent together always seemed like it went by too fast. I once told him, "I want to live forever. That is why I keep myself as healthy as possible." Instead of laughing at my naive wish, he said, "Let's do it!" Later, he told me that we should help each other live forever. Although we did not continue dating, I still cherish him as a friend.

To be honest, my life goal *is* to live forever, or at least far beyond an average life span. Do you think that I am idealistic? Would you consider me very childish?

If someone's response to your wildest dream (as long as being legal, of course) is "Let's do it!" as opposed to "Are you crazy?", you should keep that person around, at least as one of your bosom friends. This individual is on your team.

Not many people in this world can truly understand your mind. There may be many people you can have a lot of fun with, but only a limited number of people can be your soul mates. Finding someone who can read your soul is a blessing.

Switching gears, I did see some personality characteristics that I did not appreciate in some men. People are my mirrors. They reflect the qualities I like and dislike. Meeting new people is also a way to improve myself. I learn from people's merits. At the same time, I learn from those with the features I do not want to see in myself—I consciously remind myself not to cultivate those undesirable qualities.

Still, I have to be cautious when meeting new people. I once met a guy who turned out to be another person instead of the one he appeared to be. Everyone should do his/her homework before dating someone new: research this person's friend groups, occupation, current dating status, history (especially past relationships), and present relationship with his/her family. This approach is similar to an employer conducting a background check before hiring a new employee for the company.

To surmount a break-up, spend time with respectful people. They may not rescue you by dating you, but they will show you what a laudable human being is like. Then, you finally wake up from your messy dream and tell yourself: "Oh, wow! There is such an admirable person in this world, and this is an example of what I am looking for."

A desirable mate is someone capable of creating a commendable team with me—we add value to and bring out the best in each other.

*Your thoughts:

----

31. Flirtation: Adrenaline That Fuels the Relationship

Flirtation is a taste that is never boring and always alluring.

To keep a relationship fresh, you and your partner must maintain your interest in each other. Just like adding a secret ingredient to a distinctive dish, such as pepper or spice, which enhances the flavor of the food, flirtation enriches the zest in a relationship.

Managing a relationship is an art.

What is flirting, exactly? I believe that there is no standard answer, just as there is no set criterion for art. I consider it a comprehensive action, comprised of observation, attempt, reaction, seduction, imagination, and, most importantly, a sense of humor. These days, people say, **"Smart is the new sexy."** Being bright, proactive, and creative draws people's attention.

My break-up has impelled me to learn to be more skillful in a competitive society which is full of sophisticated hunters. I need to acquire flirting skills to captivate a man and unlock his heart. My flirting techniques will enable me to cast a spell designed by my own charm. A new fighter is going to be born!

*What qualities make a person attractive?

----

32. Love Is a Luxury Product

Love is an item with an exorbitant price. Expensive handbags, designer jewelry, fancy limousines, private jets, and grand mansions are nothing compared to love. They are merely background props once love appears.

Some of my friends challenged me with the belief that *love has nothing to do with money*!

I wish that were true, but nowadays, fairy tales are rare. In my experience, my financial status impacted the length of my love story. I understood that my ex wanted to find someone he could enjoy life with, not struggle. Today, the world is full of temptations. There are so many intriguing things we would like to pursue, and, unfortunately, most cost money. Even taking a class requires a fee. I would not want to bear an additional financial burden brought on by someone else. Likewise, I understand that no man would want this either. Thus, I believe that financial stability is the foundation for finding long-lasting love, because it assures that one will have the time and energy to participate in daily activities that strengthen the bond with his/her significant other.

Many years ago, I asked one of my exes, an intelligent and well-educated man, a question: "What does every man think about apart from sex?" which came from a well-known "book" (more precisely, a notebook, because it is blank inside) with a similar title. He answered right away: "**Money!**" OK, I got that. A man is actually not that complicated. If I can bring him what he wants, he is pretty simple; if I cannot, he is going to be an enigma.

I need to prepare enough capital to play the Game of Love.

To be honest, if I had not been at the lowest point in my life financially due to my start-up business, I might not have gone through this emotional crisis; then, I would not have written this book. Why? A relationship is more likely to be viable when both parties are in financial parity. As such, a relationship tends to be troubled if one party is on a far different level of comfort than the other. With a comparable financial basis, it is easier for a couple to enjoy life together in the long run.

My aborted relationship taught me that, besides the expenditure for maintaining a dynamic romance, I should retain a budget for recuperative treatments in case of an emotional crisis. Such countermeasures may include massages, outdoor activities, good food, shopping, and even a weekend getaway. This is the same concept as putting money aside for a rainy day.

Who does not want love? Yet, I have come to understand that love comes with risk. When one is in love, he/she is immersed in unique pleasure, but once that particular fountain of happiness is gone, the pain is ten times stronger than that joy.

As a person who has made a blunder in her love life, sometimes I cannot refrain from feeling disheartened. Especially during those holidays when happy couples and families are celebrating the moments, I, a loser at the Game of Love, can only run my solo show.

February 14 (Valentine's Day) is a challenging day.

Why?

Some people show off.

Many people suffer.

You may be alone, but you are not the only one.

For happy couples, every day is Valentine's Day.

As lonely singles, we are tired of watching couples kissing on social media. Come on! Give us a break!

Tormented by my break-up, I was disillusioned. I vowed to myself, "I am not going to love anyone again, except for myself. Love is too pricey to buy, and my heart, broken by love, is even more expensive to repair!"

Now, after surviving my break-up, I am once again levelheaded. As a living human being, I am still hoping that one day I will find love. I still wish to taste that sweetness again. Although I do not know how far away love is, I am putting forth efforts to pursue it. That is why I am assiduously and optimistically carrying on my life, endeavoring to advance my career, health, strength, and wisdom.

In Section 50 (What Is Love?) of Chapter XI (Appreciation of Love), I quote some interviewees' definitions of love, which are amazingly touching, sweet, and smart.

*What do you think love is?

Chapter VIII   The Sixth Sense

33.   I Pretended That He Was Not Lying

I have heard that some people have a sixth sense in a romantic relationship. I believe that I am one of them. Sometimes I fear that my worries will turn out to be correct. Many times, in my previous relationship, my intuition told me that my ex was hiding something from me, though he denied it. I swallowed this insecurity, thinking that remaining blind to the truth would prevent me from getting hurt. Later, it turned out that my doubts about him were true. He lied, repeatedly.

When someone close to you lies, you can feel it. You may have a sense that he/she is lying, but you choose to stay silent in order to keep the relationship intact. In fact, whether you believe that person depends on your willingness, not the truth. When you are in love, your feelings may defy your logical suspicions (I totally understand where you are coming from). Do not blame yourself!

As far as I can fathom, a person's sixth sense is, in a way, one's logical reasoning based on life experience. To me, if something does not make sense, I can tell right away. When I saw my ex lying to other people, I knew that he had lied to me in the same way. When I saw him intentionally ignore some text messages, I realized that he had delayed his replies to me in the same fashion. I noticed something hidden between us, but I just did not want to break the peace and expose the problem.

The sixth sense is one's innate comprehension. The study of psychology may provide you with more insight into this field. Having such knowledge can be helpful for you to manage a relationship. Regarding dating, whether you want to be honest with yourself is a matter of choice.

34. Dare You Unveil the Facts?

Life is all about options.

I was actually happier when I was "stupid." Yes, naive people tend to live a more joyful life because they are simple-minded and do not overthink. As the proverb by Thomas Gray goes, *ignorance is bliss*. Smart people's lives seem more difficult because they know and want so much. Becoming aware of the lies concealed within a relationship can be like getting struck by a thunderbolt. Dare you discover the truth?

After the break-up, I met a man whom I considered to be very intelligent and kind. I thought that he would be the one worth moving on with. We had dated for a short period of time before I got a call from a friend who advised me to stay away from him because there was something I did not know about him. I was shocked when I heard what she had to say. I thanked her and hung up the phone, stunned. Not long after, my romance with this man ended.

For weeks afterward, I felt lonely and miserable. Poor me. Why did frustration befall me again and again?

I wondered, was it a good idea to share private information about a person that might lead others to view him/her differently? Imagining that our positions were reversed, what if I knew that my friend was dating someone inappropriate? Would I tell her the hidden things that she deserved to be aware of, knowing that it would take her happiness away?

If I am not smart, let me be; if I am foolish, let me be. When I did not know the truth, I was content with my life. When I pretended to be blind, I was happy. That happiness was like a bubble that carried me in the sky, floating joyously, although it was inevitable that one day the bubble would burst and I would fall to the ground and get hurt. It would probably be a bad idea to let me fly too long and too high. Sooner or later, I would have to come back down to earth.

*Are you willing to pretend to be dumb and stay happy?

----

35. Lies and Signs—He Is Not Serious with Me

Here are common excuses and signs indicating that my partner does not take me seriously:

1. He keeps saying that he is "busy" when he is not

A friend once told me, "'Being busy' is not a convincing excuse. Even the President has time for his wife and children." Is this man really that busy the whole month that he cannot even spare a few minutes to talk to me or send a quick text? It is just a polite way to imply that he is not interested because he is not willing to make time for me.

2. No fixed time for a plan

If he does not suggest a specific time for a plan, he is pretty much saying that it is not going to happen. "Let's catch up soon" or "Let's hang out sometime" does not constitute a substantial plan. Like the wind or a cloud, these are hazy, obscure words that I just cannot grasp onto.

3. Last-minute get-together

A person tends to arrange important people and activities in his/her calendar and follow up with insignificant matters in his/her spare time.

This was my discouraging experience: my ex mostly gave me only two hours' notice when he wanted to meet up. What was that? My friends joked that I was taking a "booty call." Yes, I was just like a free service provider on demand. He did not plan a trip with me for the weekend, but only asked me to meet up with him soon because he "just happened to be free." I was not on his agenda. I was merely an object to fill a gap in his schedule.

4. He does not introduce me to his family

If I am not presented to his family, I am not considered a real dating candidate.

During the course of this unsuccessful relationship, I understood that our romantic affair was a shady deal. What was I? One item in his secret collection?

5. He does not include me in his long-term plans

If he never discusses his career goals, property planning, or wishes to have children with me, this simply means that we have no future.

Call me suspicious, but I trust my sixth sense.

I want to be honest with myself. If I feel that something is strange, my instinct is usually right about it. I can dig up the truth, or remain blind and continue with my *fake happy life*. In the long term, lies will be uncovered one day, because the truth is always there. I need to summon up the courage to face reality. Instead of wasting my time wondering and doubting, an honest conversation with my partner would be a wise option before I go too far in the wrong direction.

36. **Has He Played Enough?**

My friend, Raptor, is my career coach and one of the investors in my start-up business. As a mentor, he has continuously given me valuable advice. He is an intelligent and successful entrepreneur. As a happily married man in his fifties, he is a model husband and father, living a full life.

When I was drowning in distress, I told Raptor about my break-up. He gave me his perspective from a man's point of view—some men can move on quite easily, and it would be wise to move on gracefully. Several months later, after catching up about our business, we had an interesting conversation about my dating situation, joking about guys playing around and sharing our views toward non-serious dating:

Raptor: How's your relationship status? Any new dates?

Me: Yes, the same guy I told you about weeks ago. He has been my friend for a few years and recently we've been hanging out.

I showed Raptor a few pictures of him.

Raptor: Seems like a nice man.

Me: He makes me happy, at least. Anyway, I am currently paying attention to improving myself instead of chasing any guy.

Raptor: It seems like you never lack men chasing you. (smile emoji)

Me: Hahaha … when I become rich, I will worry even less about finding a man.

Raptor: Just like Mr. Z. (laugh emoji)

Mr. Z (whose name is not disclosed here) refers to a wealthy celebrity whose cheating scandal was widely reported throughout the media.

Me: Exactly! Guys will line up for me.

Raptor: Wow! Men rot when they get rich. It's the same for women!

Me: Men hurt me first. (laugh emoji) Well, this new date, though unlikely to be "the one," is helpful for me to recover from the break-up. In fact, he is very sociable and often goes to parties, so I know that he is not "relationship material." Nonetheless, we have many things in common. We feel comfortable together. Well, we have been friends for years, and coincidentally, we are respectively going through our recent break-ups. His presence has provided the illumination that supports me to walk out of the darkness, you know.

Even if we do not end up being a couple in the future, I hope that we will remain good friends. I can see a lot of good qualities in him. Yet, I know that women drool over him, so I am not expecting anything long-term. He could become another player.

Raptor: Players are mostly similar. Let's say there are two types of men. One type has the capability to play around with women: men who have money, good looks, free time to spare, and no wives (or are not afraid of their wives). On the other hand, men who do not have the capability to be players are the ones with no money, no good looks, or no free time, or those who respect their wives.

Me: Oh, then he's totally the type with the capability to play around! My goal is to find one without such a capability. Men who are respectful of their wives tend to be able to make a fortune— you, Raptor, are a good example.

Raptor: Many things follow the same principle. Let's look at volcanoes, for instance. Active volcanoes keep erupting until they become extinct volcanoes. Men are similar. After they have played enough, they would like to settle down. When they are no longer curious, they will want to find a partner to enjoy the rest of their lives with, peacefully.

Those potential players can be dangerous. Just because they are not capable of playing for the moment, it doesn't mean they don't want to play. Once a man possesses the power, he can turn into a player and play with fire.

Me: Hahaha! You mean Mr. Z?

Raptor: Many rich guys started from scratch. Then, after becoming financially well-off, they finally get the chance to play, unlike trust-fund babies who have been able to play around from a young age. Actually, Mr. Y, for example, could be a nice guy.

Mr. Y (whose name is not disclosed here) refers to a young celebrity who hails from a wealthy family. It has been reported in the media that he has dated a number of girls from a young age. He is known for being a "playboy."

Me: Perhaps one day, Mr. Y will become an extinct volcano. Hahaha!

Raptor: He was born rich, so he may not intend to do bad things to make a living. He is simply enjoying his dating experience.

Me: Right, he did nothing beyond hurting a few girls' feelings.

Raptor: It shouldn't be explained as "hurt" exactly. It's based on mutual benefit. It's simple. One party wants to get fame and the other wants to acquire the pleasure of romance.

Me: For the sake of preventing my future children from doing bad things under the pressure of life, I have to make adequate money first. LOL!

Our society has developed enormously, and today, a variety of opportunities exist that prolong people's dating sessions. This may hinder a lot of people from settling down. A life normally lasts only a certain number of decades, so, if a relationship does not last, it is in one's best interest to move on instead of wasting his/her time.

Raptor: Yes, there are plenty of chances for you to meet someone new. It depends on how picky you are and what you are looking for in a man. A person's primal instincts are animalistic. An animal's life is devoted to obtaining food, occupying territory, and procuring mates. For a person, this translates into acquiring possessions, assets, power, and partners. At first, one focuses on striving to pursue fortune. Then, naturally, partners come along.

My conversation with Raptor left me contemplating men. When and how can a player be tamed? It can only be done with your magic.

*Your thoughts:

----

37. How Much Cheating Can I Tolerate?

A cheater will always find a chance to cheat. Some people say that a man will either never cheat or always cheat. There is rarely "just once" when it comes to cheating. It is justified to say that loyalty requires strong self-discipline.

As mammals, humans retain two primal needs, feeding and mating, as both derive from the quest for survival.

In this modern and developed society, a lot of people do not want to miss out on anything worth trying in life. Taking this into consideration, I compromised on the fact that my ex had been dating more than one person.

After we started seeing each other, little by little, he became like an addictive drug that dragged me into a mad craving. I knew that he had been dating other women. I understood that his heart was vast and I was not the only one. I just chose to remain blind and deaf to the fact. If he did not admit it, I pretended that he was not dishonest. I was lying to myself to avoid taking on any mental stress in addition to the burden of developing my career.

I confided this unhealthy dating situation to my closest friends. Some of them agreed with my tolerance, while others did not.

Those who agreed understand that life is about balance. If no one breaks the tranquility, two lovers can enjoy harmony and focus their energy on other significant matters, such as their careers. As I mentioned previously, ignorant people live a happy life.

Those who disagreed believe that loyalty and trust form the foundation of any relationship. Cheating will eventually lead to a disaster. Why should a person waste his/her time and effort on someone who does not deserve it?

How much cheating can a person tolerate? It is a mystery.

Infidelity is such a hot topic in today's society, as temptation lies everywhere. I once saw an Internet blogger's post on social media, entitled, **"Can you tolerate cheating within a marriage?"**

There were countless interesting comments on this post. In response to the question, some people gave their forthright opinions, while others found humor in the topic. Here is some eye-catching feedback that will amuse you. You may find some of their views blunt or sad, while others may seem bold or hilarious:

A. Comments about NOT being able to tolerate cheating within a marriage:

- *To forgive him is God's business. My job is to send him to God.*

- *Cheat one time; cheat one life.*

- *Would you like to share your toothbrush with someone else?*

- *We will eventually divorce. It is just a matter of time.*

- *I had put up with it and forgiven him for several years, but I couldn't anymore, so I divorced him recently.*

- *Do those two cheaters a favor—let them be together.*

- *Rip this cheater off before dumping him/her.*

- *A cheating person is like a $100 bill that has fallen on a pile of poo—what a waste to trash it, but so gross to pick it up.*

- *Oh, no! Can you guarantee that your cheating partner is clean?*

- *Neither physical nor mental cheating is acceptable.*

B. Comments about being able to tolerate cheating within a marriage:

- *Those who are saying that they are not able to tolerate cheating are probably single. After getting married, some people begin to remain quiet.*

- *He cheats; I cheat double.*

- *For the sake of our children, I choose to be tolerant and silent.*

- *If he/she provides my children and me with an extravagant life, OK, I close my eyes and shut my mouth.*

- *It seems unforgivable, but there are many real-life cases— some of my friends have forgiven their cheating partners.*

- *I will not divorce. Let's suffer from each other. Let's see who will collapse first! (Emoji: a witty grinning face)*

- *I probably won't leave him, because someone new may be the same, or even worse.*

- *I heard my husband comment on his friend's affair, "Cheating ... is it a big deal?" I shivered.*

Has the reality surprised you?

The American Association for Marriage and Family Therapy released the following findings about infidelity on its website (updated July 2016):

"Infidelity is one of the most common presenting problems for marriage and family therapists. While the majority of couples disapprove of infidelity, some national surveys indicate that 15% of women and 25% of men have experienced intercourse outside of their long-term relationship. And, by including emotional and sexual intimacies without intercourse, these percentages increase by 20%."

I hope that you are not too astonished. Cheating in a romantic relationship is nothing new. It has existed throughout human history and will always be one of the hot topics people discuss. Neither judgment nor criticism is implied here. It is just a matter of people's lifestyle choices.

With regard to romance and love, sometimes morality and reality are not in the same orbit.

*What are your thoughts on cheating? Are you able to tolerate it?

Chapter IX   Set Free

38. Walking Away from Fear

From this break-up, I learned to be fearless.

Enslaved by the gloom arising from the termination of the relationship, I endured insomnia for months. Many times, I felt a strange tension in my heart, and I worried that I might die of fatigue, so I tried to write down everything flashing inside my head. There was sadness, anger, frustration, and depression within me. It was as though a hurricane swept through my brain and turned me into another person by destroying the old me. My mind exploded, and that was how this book was born.

Casting my memory back to my youth, when I was in high school, I kept diary entries almost every day for six years. This was because, as a teenager, I wanted to keep a log of all the feelings that derived from the experiences I had while starting to perceive the world on my own. Reading my adolescent diary now as an adult, I am amazed every time—wow, that was how I thought and felt then! The records are fascinating to me, but I keep them only for myself.

Then, as a young adult, I wrote some poems and songs, hoping that one day they would become my legacy. Songs are the most shareable and immortal medium available to us; anyone can sing them, anytime and anywhere. The lyrics of a song tell a story or convey a message, floating alongside a melody—the integration of lyrics and melody generates a beautiful piece of artwork. Such a combination reflects the creator's emotion and resonates with singers and audiences. How magical creativity is!

Now, with this book, I am trying to be brave and candid (I do not mean that I am crazy or indecent). I want my thoughts to be relatable to people, and I hope that my readers can benefit from it.

If I do not speak up now, I may never get another chance to in my lifetime.

One thing in this world with no boundaries is creativity. You can be creative anytime and all the time!

Set your mind free and create anything you are fond of! Do it whenever you feel inspired. Do not hesitate. It is a delightful process. Every little thing you do will eventually reward you.

I hope to try everything meaningful to me during my finite existence in the world. I want to excel. I want to stand out. I desire to leave something in this world that will outlast me.

Now, I let my emotions flow freely instead of suppressing them:

Cannot sleep? Stay awake.

Want to cry? Let the tears fall.

Like many of you, I always long to find love, but I must love myself first because no one else will adore me as much as I do.

Have you ever had the experience of being so attached to one person that you cannot escape? It feels like your heart is chained to this person. This is dangerous because it can be the source of heartbreak if that relationship cracks.

Love is something powerful, yet complicated. When you are infatuated with someone, you do things beyond your sanity, pulled in by adoration beyond your awareness.

I have to say that we are born with the inclination to pursue love. Here is a story that illustrates the fact that love is universally desired. As a service provider for content creators, I have been managing the official page of a popular dog on social media. I once posted the following caption on behalf of the dog:

It feels so good being loved (with a picture depicting the dog's owner rubbing the dog's chest).

Surprisingly, this post collected thousands of likes, comments, and shares.

I was amazed! This sentiment crossed my mind in a flash of inspiration! I thought that I was thirsty for love. Actually, I was not the only one.

This caption resonated with so many people. I realized that many of us want to be loved, on different levels and to different extents.

I have learned that courage is the key to setting my mind free to love myself, my life, and the world we live in.

Life is like fireworks, which burn for a limited time, so let your life shine!

*Describe your most fearless moments:

It's All About Dreams

Have you ever thought of something unrealistic?
Don't you ever think it's just your interest
But I'm gonna make it a bit dramatic
As I know of some kind of magic

I'm living in a house where we live on our dreams
We're dying for something that got us fascinated
Survival against our masterpieces
I'm gonna step up
Now here it is

Oh it's all about dreams
What do you think?

Let's try the word motivation
All I need is your inspiration
Whenever life is a contradiction
Let my drive follow my emotion

*My soul my heart I beg you give me one chance, please
*It's screwed; it's cracked. I hope you listen to me
*How my stomach was filled
*How my castle was built
*Is it true? Is it real?
*It's all about dreams.

39. <u>Who Am I?</u>

Ever since I was a little girl, I have been asking myself these questions:

Why am I me?

Why am I here?

Why do I think in my own way?

I can talk to myself and picture incredible scenes in my mind. Is it just me, or everybody?

I am an atheist and I always believe in science, but still, so many things remain unknown in this universe and it leaves me wondering. When I was younger, my understanding was that a living creature is a group of substances. Now, I have begun doubting whether I have a soul inside my body. Does reincarnation exist? Although I do not believe in it, I hope that it does exist because I want to stay in this world for good (I have imagined that I would return as a dog).

Am I just a bunch of chemical reactions that have formed an organic human body? What am I, ultimately? Very often, I ask myself, "Am I real? Are things around me virtual? What exactly dominates my body?"

My final question is:

What on earth is the force inside me that drives me to feel so attached to my ex?

For a year after the break-up, I was eager to figure out what ruled my mind and body, because I was dying to expel my anguish, the souvenir of my doomed relationship.

I also feel that there is a power within me that grows from my endurance and self-healing. This must be what people refer to as WILLPOWER.

Willpower and independence are two crucial qualities for one to disentangle from emotional turmoil.

My willpower is the source of energy for my actions.

My independence is my capability to:

1. Enjoy being by myself—I am able to appreciate my own time and make it productive when I am alone; and

2. Count on myself—without asking for help, I can manage my life.

Following my break-up, I began spending more time thinking about myself, the life I am living, and my position in this world. Recalling the joy of keeping a journal when I was a teenage girl, now I have picked up writing again. I think. I write. I think. I rewrite ... systematically forming my fragmented thoughts into organized words. This process allows me to put myself back together during my journey toward healing.

Attempting to escape from the sorrow that sprang from the haunting memories of my ex, I have delved deeper into the enigma of "me."

I want to decode *what* I am.

*Do you keep thinking about who you are?

----

40. <u>Psychology and Me</u>

Recovering from my break-up, I realized that I did not understand myself as much as I thought I did, so I was intrigued to learn more about psychology.

A person is a complex system. The mind's inner workings are tremendously wondrous.

Psychology is the study of the mind and behavior. It has always been a fascinating subject to me.

My break-up made me feel so ashamed of myself because I could not believe that I was so affected by it. My self-esteem was wounded badly. Thus, I wanted to manage myself better. I also desired to understand how other people think and act so that I would be able to improve my ability to deal with them.

The more I digested, the more I realized how much remained out there for me to explore. My body is an organism formed by millions of chemical reactions, and my brain is the control panel. Looking to psychology for answers, I began searching for more insights about the body and mind to fix myself after being wrecked by my break-up.

The path of overcoming my sadness taught me an important principle: **unconditional acceptance**. I had no choice but to accept the fact that our lives, his and mine, were no longer connected, regardless of how I felt. The only thing that I could change was my attitude. I could cry pathetically at home every day, or I could take action to propel my life into a better state.

Knowing my body is the first step to knowing my mind. Why do break-ups hurt so much? When I went through my own, it felt as though a part of me, with which I had built a strong connection, had been amputated.

Some people compare break-ups to drug withdrawal. Biochemically, a romantic relationship pumps a good amount of dopamine into your brain, causing you to feel happier than usual. Your significant other, thereby, becomes a distinctive source of your dopamine. This effect is similar to what an addictive drug generates. When a break-up with this significant other occurs, this happiness is gone because this unique source of dopamine has departed. Your body can react by feeling sick, weak, and even depressed.

In this case, you may want to replace your former source of dopamine with another. That was why I made efforts to create break-up songs, write this book, meet nice people, and focus on my career. New happiness produced fresh blood in my life.

As a layman, I have found that the following books are great reads for those interested in learning about the human mind, human behavior, and the psyche: *Psychology and Life* by Richard Gerrig and *Psychology For Dummies* by Adam Cash.

You will be even more productive if you come to your own understanding regarding the study of the mind—you will become better at observing people and analyzing their behaviors. It is a new level of growth.

Life is a learning process. Enjoy!

*Do you know yourself well enough?

---

41. Building My Name into a Brand

When I was a child, I was shy, timid, and unsociable. Now, as an adult, my mentality has changed. I want to be known; I want to be remembered.

I hope to establish my name as a brand, which is an asset. Everyone's name, whether small or big, has a reputation.

Little by little, step by step, year after year, my name has become known. I have developed relationships with my peers, friends, and colleagues from school, work, and social activities. These relationships and my image of being a reliable person are my intangible assets that cannot be replaced. When people mention me, I hope that they speak with appreciation, because I have worked heart and soul to build up my name with every little thing I have done.

With today's communication technology, my interactions with this world are becoming even broader. For example, on LinkedIn, my career path is presented; on Instagram and Facebook, users get to know my personality and lifestyle through my posts; on Twitter, my opinions can be heard. I am able to reach out to and stay in touch with people around the world with social media.

Now, I am no longer shy. Just like many of you, I am proud of the person I am, so I am happy to be publicly recognized.

Branding my name is my goal. To achieve this requires self-discipline and persistence: I try to avoid doing stupid things; I stay empathetic toward others; I act with good intentions; I keep refining myself; I plan things for the long-term.

Keeping my life in the public eye is another way to remain compliant with my code of conduct.

I enjoy people's attention, appreciation, and admiration, but I know that they do not come for free. I have to earn them.

A good reputation is not easy to "construct," but it is very easy to crack. With one single mistake, a person's reputation can be quickly and permanently destroyed. This notion is also discussed in Section 75 (Reputation: Hard to Build, Easy to Break) of Chapter XIV (How Much These Types of Value Mean to Me).

During my limited time in this world, I strive to **develop my reputation, an intangible asset that will outlast my human body**.

*How much does your reputation matter to you?

Chapter X   What We Can Learn from Farewells

42. Farewells to Our Pets

The relationship with my ex was not the only thing that I lost. I, unfortunately, kissed my dog goodbye five months before my heartbreak over him. It was an utterly painful time for me, enduring first the loss of my dog and then the relationship.

My song "You Will Always Be Remembered" at the beginning of Chapter XI (Appreciation of Love) was written to memorialize my dog, Shanelle, after she died from an accident when she was almost ten years old. I experienced tremendous sadness witnessing her suffering for a week before she finally passed away. I will never forget petting her body on the veterinarian's table the night she left me for good. I have shed more tears over her accident and passing than all the other losses in my life combined.

Three important things I have learned from the loss of my dog:

Life is so fragile.

Accidents can happen anytime, anywhere, in any way.

Love someone before it is too late.

Shanelle from one week old to fully grown, and her mom Mico

Shanelle and me

Shanelle had always been very healthy and energetic, so the last thing I expected was that she would die after overeating dog food at one time from the automatic feeder followed by chicken bones that my mom gave her as a treat. This combination severely injured her stomach and intestines (please allow me to remind you that chicken bones are very dangerous for dogs!). Even though the veterinarian performed surgery to save her, it was ultimately not enough.

The hardest part for me was watching her suffer for a week before she finally let go. She vomited shortly after every light meal. I worried the entire time because I knew she was in pain. Although the veterinarian told me that he had put painkillers in her intravenous fluids, I still felt so helpless knowing that there was nothing I could do.

During the week when she was sick and receiving medication, she was very calm, curled into a tight little ball. She had never been so quiet. It was like a truck running over my heart the whole time. I tried to withhold my tears in front of everyone but could not help weeping when I was alone.

The veterinarian took tender care of her, and even stayed with her in the pet clinic overnight for several nights before and after her surgery. Three days after her surgery, he called me when I was at work, gently informing me, "She has a fever now and you have to be prepared in case anything happens." I was shocked at that moment. The worry overwhelmed me the entire day. I went to see her in the evening right after work. She got very excited the moment she saw me, even though I could tell that her body was very weak. My heart bled when I saw her pale lips and labored breathing. After I played with her about an hour, the veterinarian told me to go home and let her rest. Reluctantly, I left.

Two hours later, around eleven pm, the veterinarian called me. With a tremble in his voice, he told me, "I am so sorry, but her heart stopped beating, despite everything I did." I ran to the pet clinic right away, sobbing and shaking all the way. When I got there, she was on the doctor's table, lying still. I was stunned. Except for crying, I could not do anything. My body felt as if it were frozen and my head felt like it was exploding, but it was also a relief for me in a way because I knew now she would not suffer anymore. The veterinarian was very sad and sorry. I knew that he had done his best. I was grateful to him for his care and support. No one could have predicted that freak accident.

He said to me, "We will have to put her in a box later." In tears, I asked, "She's still warm. Can we wait until her temperature goes down?" He said, "Sure." We stood petting her for about an hour, the very last time I could touch her softly. Still, I understood that it was not her anymore—her soul was gone and only her body was left. She was no longer here with me.

She was my first pet, and this was the first time I experienced losing a close companion. Watching and touching her body, I was still not able to accept what had happened. The only thoughts that entered my mind were of those moments of her being excited and energetic. I only wished that she could wake up and lick my fingers once again, but her body just gradually became cool and rigid. I could not believe she was gone so suddenly. I realized that a life could end at any time, unexpectedly. What could I do after she was already gone? Nothing. The veterinarian told me that she was in heaven now, where she had no pain and only happiness.

On the other hand, I was glad that she had been happy and healthy her whole ten years while living with my family, ever since I took her home at just one month old. She had a life filled with love and care, and she loved and cared for us. She had played with me not long before her heart stopped beating. I hoped that she was happy in the last moments of her life. I believed that she was finally at peace and would not suffer anymore. All I had to do was let go.

Since her death, I keep reminding myself:

Love someone in time.

Do what is meaningful to you before it is too late.

While I was writing this section on several quiet nights, I kept weeping while typing. It brought back so many memories and feelings. Even though more than a year had passed, I could still remember her scent, how it felt when I was caressing her head, her ears, her back, her tummy, and her paws, how it felt when she was licking my fingers, how she cleverly reacted to my commands ... It all seemed like it happened yesterday. My recollections were still fresh and clear. It was really devastating to know that she would never ever come back to me.

Today, I still think of her every now and then, especially when I am alone. Sometimes, I see her in my dreams, where we mostly enjoy a fun time together. It is not about dwelling on the past, but about what we have learned from the experience and what we arrange for the future.

What kind of dog was she?

I would describe her as a little person instead of a little dog because she could interact with me so well and had been so sweet to our family. Guarding the family was in her nature. I had many of the best times of my life with her—she showed me the beauty of companionship. I will elaborate on this in Chapter XI (Appreciation of Love).

43. Farewells to Our Families

I do not hate anyone in this world, but there is one person I can never forgive because he disappointed my mother, my siblings, and me so much: my father.

My father, who taught me how to be a decent person, was a good husband to my mother until I turned seven, when my parents started a small business, a clothing store. Benefitting from Mom's diligence and capability, my parents began making an income from the steady growth of the family business. Unexpectedly, after becoming financially a little better off, my father turned into another person. He rarely came home. He seldom spent time with me or my newborn sister and brother. He neglected my grandmother, an elderly lady. He was cheating on Mom with another woman, or maybe multiple women. Without making any contribution to the family, he asked Mom for money, as he was spending lavishly on his other businesses. He even incurred debts that Mom had to pay off for him.

Mom was always fighting with him, day and night, about him not coming home, asking for money once back home, cheating with other women, spending money on other women, losing money from his businesses, never taking care of his children, etc. I was thoroughly overwhelmed by witnessing these quarrels for seven years from the age of seven.

Once, Mom threw the telephone onto the wall right after she picked up a call, from a strange woman looking for "her husband," my father. On one occasion when I was ten years old, my school friend told me in a teasing tone, "I saw your dad on the street the other day, with a woman in his arms, but not your mom." These words left me speechless, and I pretended to be fine while I was extremely embarrassed and hurt. Crazy things never stopped disrupting our life. Countless sleepless nights and nightmares devastated us.

Finally, when I was fourteen, Mom divorced him and became a single mother with three children. In 1996, divorce was very rare in China. It took enormous courage for Mom to officially split with him. It was a tough move for our family because my little brother and sister were only seven and eight years old respectively. Although we had tried every option to remain a complete family, we could no longer tolerate him. We had to end it regardless of the pain.

I cannot even remember when I last saw him. I prepared a birthday gift for him, an artistically designed notebook, hoping that he would smile when he received it, but I never had the chance to hand it to him because he never showed up.

Not long after Mom's divorce, I had one phone call with him and that was our last conversation. Now, I only remember one thing I said to him:

"You don't appreciate what you have!"

That was it. That was the farewell I had with my father, a phone call with one unhappy statement.

It was such a disaster for a kid to go through.

Nevertheless, since then, Mom and her three children have been enjoying a peaceful life. Later, Mom met a warm-hearted man who became her boyfriend and we all get along well.

Breaking up with a parent is very bitter, especially at a young age. The break-up was the result of a huge disappointment. After all that we had struggled with, I preferred ending our father-daughter relationship to continuing it with endless resentment and fear. Missing a parent is tough, but it has driven me to be a more resilient person.

It has been more than twenty years since Mom's divorce. I have asked her several times, "Do you regret marrying him?"

"No," Mom always replied. "I still appreciate that I had three children with him and then created my career. I became a self-made woman because he did not provide me with a comfortable life. We moved to this new city together and I have built my life here. Although he changed, he left me with a challenge that impelled me to strive harder to achieve my goals. I still wish him the best."

Mom is so magnanimous about this unsuccessful marriage. She is a brave and independent woman. She has always been my role model. She has accepted all the challenges in her life without wasting time complaining. With the income she earned through painstakingly running her clothing stores, she raised her three children by herself—took care of us when we were sick, educated us, and sent all of us to college.

How could Mom imagine that her husband would become irresponsible after the third child was born? Instead of staying miserable or asking for help, she survived all the adversities that befell her. She has earned everything she deserves in her life: her income as well as our love and respect.

Although I bade farewell to my father, I have never felt like I am missing a parent because Mom has been great enough. Her life has proven to me:

Challenges may arise anytime. Do not fear.

44. __Farewells to Our Friends__

One of my girlfriends, Carol, deeply impressed me with her indomitable attitude toward living while battling a rare disease.

Carol is a beautiful, attractive, and classy woman. She always shows up with a sunshine smile. We met six years ago in Los Angeles, and we hung out pretty often. She was very familiar with the city, so she took me to parties, shows, restaurants, and spas. We got along very well, and we had many things in common, especially working on creative projects. In short, we understood each other's goals and souls.

Unfortunately, she has been fighting an uncommon chronic disease for years while trying different medications, even though she is fit and maintains a healthy vegetarian diet.

Despite the illness, she has been living her life optimistically all along. She has traveled around the world to give speeches about women's empowerment. She has planned a TV show with professionals about her extraordinary life experiences. She has kept up with fashionable styles. From her appearance, people would never believe that she has been suffering from a chronic disease.

She has a special ability to detect people's inner energy. On one occasion, she tried to sense the power inside me. I tried saying my name in different tones, volumes, and languages, as well as different things about myself, but my energy had not reached its peak. Then, as soon as I stated the name of the company I had founded, "EnterChance," she responded that my energy field became the strongest! We were thrilled and screamed out, "Yes!" It made sense! I had put my greatest effort and all my savings into my start-up company. At that moment, I realized how much this new business meant to me. That day, we had a heartening talk about the excitement and hardship of running toward our dreams.

Besides my career, she knew about my unsuccessful romantic relationship the whole time. She was one of the few friends who did not oppose my unofficial relationship with my ex before the break-up. Every time she heard my unpleasant stories, she told me, "You don't know what will happen in your life. Just enjoy the time with him and keep your eyes open."

We hung out at least once a year until two years ago, when her health situation declined so dramatically that she had to go back to her home country to receive medical attention. We still keep in touch through messages. I told her about my break-up, as she has always been my loyal listener. She told me that ending a relationship is just one of the footsteps in a lifetime expedition. Compared with her life-threatening health issues, a break-up is nothing.

A year ago, I asked her about her status. She told me that she was too weak to walk and had lost some weight. She had been spending most of her time in bed. She communicated with friends only through her computer because she did not want to be seen in this condition. I suggested I visit her and assured her that I would not judge. Sadly, she told me that she had lost her voice and was not able to talk, but she was already very delighted that we could chat by messaging and go through our old photos. When I heard this from her, my heart ached.

I do not know when we can have a reunion. I hope that she will take a favorable turn soon so that we will have a chance to get together like before.

Notwithstanding her health condition, she continues to post motivational words on social media. Her life is full of stories. She has been making a continuous effort to inspire others. Every time I see her new posts, I am so happy, but I also have mixed feelings.

It is really sad that I do not know when I can see this close friend in person again. Meanwhile, I understand that every day, I, too, am one step closer to my final destination, so I should be grateful that I wake up breathing every morning.

45. Farewells to Our Employers

In terms of relationships, the first one is the most special. One's first job is like his/her first love.

Regarding the "break-up" with my employer, let me share with you the two versions of the farewell letter I sent to my colleagues at PwC Shenzhen Office, my first employer, on my last day after working there for seven years:

Farewell Letter—regular version:

August 12, 2012

My dear friends,

Today is my last day at PwC, but it is absolutely not the last day of our friendship.

I feel so proud that for the past seven years I have worked with the most intelligent, capable, and outstanding people I have ever met. I have been blessed to have had the experience of standing on the shoulders of the giant, which is what we know as the PwC Experience (put aside the real definition for the moment ... this is just how I feel now :P). It is not only how proud of all of you I am, but also that I am honored (truly, madly, deeply) to be one of you, among your people, your world, your legend. If the universe follows the rule of equation, my understanding is that the calories I have burned here have become my monthly salary, my confidence, and your trust in me!

It is so hard to express my endless gratitude to everyone here, because it would be comprised of many long paragraphs, and it would for sure be inefficient (you all taught me to be efficient!). In this case, I would like to present my overall appreciation to all of you as a whole, to give a true and fair reflection of the state of my feelings. Thank you all!!! (Please imagine a big hug from me at this point!)

Well, realistically, for those peers in the office whom I have not yet treated to lunch (well, please do not be mad at me ...), how about an alternative—you will get a piece of chocolate or candy from my desk! Enjoy the energy from the sugar and refresh yourselves for a moment (limited, first come first served ^_^). Then, forget about my secret drawer filled with the evil you-know-what (SNACKS).

Seriously, please let me know about any upcoming event— lunch, dinner, conference, etc. We are always connected. I am always excited to hear about your news!

I wish you all the best!

Florence Chow

Farewell Letter—poem version:

August 12, 2012

My Kings and My Queens,

Seven years where I have been,

Not the peace,

Not the ease,

But the battles under your lead,

From the acknowledgment of receipt or the LOE*,

To the deliverables that I can tweet,

How many deadlines that we could not miss,

How many milestones that we have reached,

Got no tears, bore no fears,

Got stronger from your cheers,

I send my gratitude to my buddies, coaches, and "coachees,"

Let me know about the events, gatherings, or feasts,

Last but not least,

Wish that you will always be happy, healthy, and RICH!

Yours sincerely,

Florence, once worked at PwC

*LOE means letter of engagement.

Many of my colleagues replied to me with WOWs and blessings. Some of them told me that they saved my farewell e-mail. One even responded to me, "Now, I've got a new template for a farewell letter!"—such a compliment.

Getting employed is like getting married.

You bind yourself to someone legally, to work together, learn together, and achieve something together. You build a relationship and develop mutual trust with this partner. It could be for a short period, a long time, or even a lifetime.

Having a good employer is like marrying the right person. You feel that every day is enriched and you are growing up together with this companion. You are not only earning money every month, but also creating value for yourself, including your knowledge, capability, and confidence. Your ambition is deployed and your goal can be attained.

Resigning from employment can be like a divorce.

Not every break-up is unhappy. When you truly love your employer, you will feel happy about the resignation. I had made the decision to resign from PwC Shenzhen Office a year before I finally did. I planned to step down from the position because I would be thirty years old. I intended to devote myself to creative writing in my thirties, switching from a secure profession to a brand-new venture. I was willing to take a risk and pursue my passion after establishing a financial foundation because I had always aspired to commit myself to creative writing, such as writing songs, books, and movie scripts. I hoped to compose something shareable that could outlast my time in this world.

My first resignation was bittersweet. For two weeks before my last day at the firm, I had been hanging out with different departments and project teams at my farewell lunches and dinners. I loved my job, my company, and the people there, who had been my respected teachers, mentors, and buddies. I was appreciative of the opportunity to collaborate with so many brilliant and competent professionals. There were no painful tears at this break-up, only joyful conversations and laughter before we went our separate ways.

Of course, we had been through a lot of hard yet meaningful times together while carrying out our duties. In those days, we teamed up and devoted ourselves to completing intensive auditing projects. Challenges came up all the time, but we always found ways to accomplish the missions perfectly. Our diligent work was recorded in heavy piles of documents with comments and remarks. Those seven years were just like a movie to me. I can still remember the training classes I attended as a learner and later as an instructor, the glamorous scenes at every annual dinner, and the first project I was assigned to in 2005, during which I started acquiring knowledge and skills from my senior colleagues.

It was my happiest break-up ever! Actually, we are not exactly broken up because I still hang out with my peers every year at dinner gatherings and events. I follow the company on social media. I am invited to the alumni activities every year. To me, our bond remains intact.

Experience is the best teacher.

Isn't it fabulous to truly love your job and your company? Try not to simply think about what tough duties the job entailed, but rather recognize what value the job instilled in you. Then, you will know from where your appreciation comes.

Even if you had some unpleasant experiences with your former or current employer, you can still be thankful for what you have learned, the network you have built, and how much you have grown from the position. You can always consider the "break-up" with your employer an amicable goodbye. Despite the conclusion of employment, the friendship will continue.

*What do you like about your job?

----

*What do you dislike about your job but are able to overcome?

----

46. Farewells to Our Comfort Zones

All my life, I have been longing to do something creative. When I turned thirty, I felt that I was ready to embark on a new vocation based on my enthusiasm, so I said farewell to my first employer. Then, I started my own business to produce songs and short travel videos.

Before sharing those exciting moments about my start-up company, let me be honest with you:

How quickly a start-up business can destroy a person's life!

Let me explain to you how much of a struggle my life has become since the commencement of my start-up:

1. Financial crisis

The more I work, the poorer I become. I have spent all my savings because I believe in my business. Then, I use my credit card to pay and defer my bills by installment. This is similar to the snowball effect. I am expecting to make a good income in the future, so I am brave enough to incur debts in the present.

Maybe I have created an illusion for myself, but I am holding onto a belief, which is the source of my persistence in chasing my goal. I have convinced myself that my financial crisis is just a temporary situation. However, nothing about the future is guaranteed. No one, including myself, can tell me when I will start to make a decent return on investment. Only one thing is certain: my credit card bill will arrive every month!

If a person is not financially flexible, a start-up business is an absolute nightmare! Beware!

2. Mental pressure

When one person tells you that a start-up business may "overwhelm" your life, you probably respond: "You may not understand me, but I'll make it work."

If more than three people tell you that a start-up business may "ruin" your life, you cannot help panicking. When your family and friends start advising you to be realistic and get a reliable job, you may begin doubting yourself.

That is just one of the many challenges stemming from a start-up. People question me. I question myself. Every day is full of unknowns. I spend a lot of time in an anxiety whirlpool, wondering why it has not worked yet, why life is so tough on me, and whether I have underestimated the risk of a start-up.

Sometimes, I blame myself for getting into this difficult situation. I avoid talking to my family and friends about it. When I see people's fabulous lives on social media, I think less of myself. My mind is in conflict—sometimes immersed in a great motivation to do something fulfilling, other times under high pressure, wondering why my projects have not taken off.

The more stressed I get, the more hair I shed. Sometimes, I cannot fall asleep. Very often, I do not pay enough attention to my diet. I have noticed the unfavorable changes in my body. I cannot deny that I am getting weaker and older.

My start-up leaves my mind and body exhausted.

3. Loneliness

First of all, I have invested most of my time and savings in the new business, so I do not have as much leisure as others. I have neither time nor the inclination for dating. I am staying distant from my friends.

Secondly, I do not confide how much I have tried but failed to my family and friends. I dare not. I do not want to burden my family with my plight, and I am afraid to look incompetent in front of my friends.

Thirdly, I do not disclose the details of what I am doing because I do not want my ideas to be stolen.

I am handling a lot of difficulties by myself. Loneliness is my company.

Overall, a start-up business demands one's financial foundation, determination, and perseverance.

So, why am I still doing this?

My dream is the fuel for my career. In the hope of realizing this vision, I endeavor to create something from scratch, like building a castle with every single brick.

The beauty of a start-up business is that the possibility is a mystery.

It is about a belief.

It is in the future tense.

People often respond to me, "Wow! Such a great idea!" That is all they can say.

Nothing is promised. To give up would be so easy, but I constantly reassure myself that my persistence will lead me to a successful outcome one day.

Sometimes, I question myself; sometimes, I doubt myself; sometimes, I disagree with myself.

Still, I embolden myself:

If mankind had not kept innovating all along, this world would not have become as civilized and marvelous as it is today. Those brave hearts reap the fruits from their harvests.

Leaving my comfort zone is an enormous challenge.

If you are planning to start something new, that is exciting— **seize the opportunity to thrive!**

Make sure that you are financially and emotionally ready.

Explain yourself to your family and your team. They will be your biggest support.

Enjoy the course of creativity! Life is short, so make yourself shine. Worst case, you will come back to square one and try again. In an ideal scenario, wisdom, experience, and happiness will be your fortune.

Holding onto a prosperous vision fills you with satisfaction!

*Are you going to put more effort into what you are passionate about?

Chapter XI   Appreciation of Love

47. <u>You Will Always Be Remembered</u>

To memorialize my beloved dog, Shanelle, I modified an old song, "Now He's Someone Else's Baby" written after a break-up in 2013, and turned it into a new one, "You Will Always Be Remembered."

You Will Always Be Remembered

You were my best friend, and will always be
You brought me happiness in the days you danced with me

You were my angel, and will always be
You left me a legacy; time won't change a thing

You brought out the best in me
You're always in my memory

You showed me love
You taught me love
You gave me the love
You were just my loved one
As if you were with me, always with me

*You will always be remembered
*Your existence has become the source of my power
*I understand that my life goes on
*You will always be remembered

48. Love Before It Is Too Late

"You Will Always Be Remembered" was originally a sad song that conveyed the feelings related to a painful break-up. After losing Shanelle in October of 2017, as I mentioned in Section 42 (Farewells to Our Pets), I changed some lyrics and made it into a new song that expressed love, as I believed that it would be more valuable to appreciate love.

Following Shanelle's death, I was in a state of deep sorrow for months. I still have not gotten over it. What I have learned from losing her will affect me for the rest of my life:

Life is so delicate. Love someone before it is too late.

Is it ever really too late? I keep reminding myself, "It is never too late to take action." Time may have passed, but it is not too late yet.

49. What I Learned About Love from My Dog

I always considered my dog, Shanelle, as my child, because we were able to communicate very well and had built a strong connection. She understood my commands and could express her needs to me. She was an impeccably trained dog. Because of her, I was a proud mama. I hope that I will have children with whom I can build a bond just as solid as the one I had with her.

Caring for and guarding the family was her nature.

Shanelle was a Poodle-Chihuahua mix. My best friend Sharon's dog, Mico, gave birth to five lovely puppies during Christmas of 2007. When the puppies were one month old, Sharon called me and excitedly requested: "Please come take a baby. They are growing up so quickly, and we cannot handle them anymore! Hahaha!"

I was exhilarated! I had always wanted to have a dog for myself but had never decided to get one because I had been focusing on my studies and then work. At that moment, I was ready to welcome a puppy into my life as my career had become stable. My brother and I went to Sharon's home right after work. We were thrilled by Mico and her five adorable puppies, all of which were actively stumbling around. We joyfully played together for an hour. I already had the type in mind, so I said to Sharon, "I want the quietest girl here." She handed me Shanelle. "This is the one!"

Shanelle was the fourth dog in the litter. The first three newborns were larger and more energetic. The fourth and fifth were smaller and meeker. This was in accordance with the laws of nature. I wanted a dog with a tractable disposition, so that it would be easier for my family to manage.

I wrapped her in the detachable hood of my winter jacket and went home. She was excited and curious, wagging her tail as soon as she arrived in my bedroom. I chose the name Shanelle (pronounced like "Chanel") from the first three letters of her first handler's name, Sharon. Shanelle responded to her name right away, so we knew that we had picked the right one. After playing around and having a meal, she slept comfortably inside my scarf with a few dolls around in her bed.

It proved to me that she was not only obedient, as I had hoped, but also very smart and sweet.

On her second day living with me, I placed her in her dog bed after a meal. She tried to get out, so I put her in a basket instead, afraid that I might step on her. She still kept trying to escape, so I finally relented and let her out. Right away, she went to pee on a laid-out newspaper. At that moment, I realized that she had been trying to get out to pee the whole time. I felt terribly sorry that I did not get her message sooner. She was such a sensible puppy who did not want to mess up her bed. I came to understand that I should learn more about her body language and establish mutual communication.

In a week, she learned to sit before she was allowed to eat. Following that, she started to be obedient and follow our new commands. Later, she was trained to lie down, stay, come, give her left paw and right paw, get the ball, jump, hurdle, roll, and go to bed. She was always the entertainer in high spirits whenever we had guests. Everyone loved her so much and enjoyed her company.

The winter she was born was a freezing cold one. As she was so little and delicate, I kept her near the heater in my bedroom most of the time. She was gentle and quiet, but I could see the curiosity in her eyes. She came to my bed, wagging her tail to greet me every morning once I awakened. To this day, I still wonder how she could tell the moment I woke up. Maybe she smelled my morning breath?

She was our little home guardian. She would lie next to whomever was sleeping. She was the first to say hello to everyone in the morning. We lived in an apartment, and whenever a stranger passed by our unit, she would be there at the door, listening and sniffing carefully. She was always the "leading" one to warmly greet whomever came home or visited. She was never lazy. With her, we did not need a doorbell.

She was a proactive protector of anyone who appeared to be in a poor situation in the family—we were so amused to see her backing up whomever was being scolded by Mom. At home, Mom and my little sister had conflicts over trivial matters pretty often. Whenever Mom was complaining to my sister about her mistakes, Shanelle would walk slowly to my sister, then sit next to her, staring at Mom, as if she were begging Mom to forgive my sister. No one could help laughing at this point—her sweetness melted our hearts! She was just like a little mediator at home. Regardless of whatever had happened, she just wanted to defend whichever family member was in trouble.

Shanelle was very easygoing. Mom was not a huge fan of dogs originally, but she grew to love Shanelle like her own child. Shanelle had the qualities any mom could appreciate: she loved fruit and vegetables, and she was not picky with food. She enjoyed our healthy homemade meals every day—green leaves, celery, broccoli, carrots, apples, pears, watermelon, and blueberries were all her favorites. She was also crazy about yogurt, so we let her lick the container clean. Whenever Mom showed her a bone, she would get extremely excited and could roll on the floor on command more than ten times before finally getting her reward.

She was playful yet disciplined. It was mostly Mom who took care of her. To reduce Mom's workload, we kept Shanelle inside all the time (like a cat), so that she would not beg to go out. With her docile temperament, she was totally fine with staying inside.

When she was bored, she intentionally played with her toys in front of us to invite us to interact with her. Once in a while, she messed up the sofa by jumping around when we were all out. The moment we were back home, she admitted her guilt right away by showing a submissive posture (four legs toward the sky) with her eyes wide open. Because of her honesty, we did not have the heart to punish her. Even during the long, boring days, she would only dishevel the sofa, but never damaged anything. Her harmless naughtiness was actually endearing.

Even when she was receiving medical treatment at the pet clinic, as I mentioned in Section 42 (Farewells to Our Pets), Shanelle was calm and well-behaved. She never barked or struggled. She knew that she was getting help and was completely cooperative. The veterinarians and the staff were impressed by her gentleness. Unfortunately, these were her last days with us. All her life, she never brought us any trouble. Pure love was what she delivered.

I have learned a lot from her:

1. Love someone if you want to.

   We lived together for ten years and there was not a single day I did not feel her love. She was always on the front line to protect us—guarding was her instinct. She asked for nothing in return. I was glad that she had enjoyed her entire life except the last week, when she was ill due to an unimaginable accident.

   Tomorrow is not guaranteed, so love someone without delay.

2. If you want something, all you need to do is ask. Be bold.

3. Loyalty is a kind of beauty.

4. Conflict is not allowed at home.

5. Stay curious.

6. Less is more: less desire, more happiness.

Reviewing my life, why am I ever unhappy? I already know the answer—I have too many desires, so I cannot truly be happy until I achieve them all. My dog was far simpler than this. Our family was all she needed. As long as we were together, she was content—simple food and living conditions, just a simple life would be good enough. If I demand less from life, I will be much happier. That is why people say: *less is more.*

*What kinds of beauty and virtue do you see in your loved ones?

----

50. <u>What Is Love?</u>

What is love? This is a good question. Frankly speaking, love is something magical that can drive me out of my mind!

Love is a force so powerful that it is able to make a person willing to surrender everything for it. Dramatic love stories always move me to tears. One of my favorite movie quotes comes from *Alita: Battle Angel*, when Alita says to Hugo:

"We don't belong anywhere, except together."

With a loved one, every day is Valentine's Day.

With a loved one, all odds can be vanquished.

To make a video about the definition of love, I once interviewed many couples at the annual Gay Pride parade in West Hollywood, California. I asked each couple one simple question: **"What is love?"** I was amazed by their perspectives on the meaning of LOVE. Here are some of my favorite answers:

- *Love is caring for someone beyond all rationality. The feelings for someone drive you crazy.*

- *Love is when someone is just irresistible to you.*

- *Expressing the feelings you have for someone and showing him/her you love him/her—it's the biggest emotion that a person could have for another person.*

- *Love is ... having someone who is behind you 100% and loves you unconditionally, no matter what you're going through.*

- *Love is undying affection and patience, and ... you know, long nights with wine and pizza.*

- *God, I don't know ... I think love is more like the indescribable emotions you have in life. It's an investment (his friend beside him said, "This is a good explanation."), being willing to invest in someone for love—I know it sounds financial, but you know it is an INVESTMENT!*

- *Love is whatever you feel comfortable with, whatever you feel with your best friend.*

- *Love is, you know that feeling, like you want to do something for somebody, just because you want to. It's like, you love your mom. You buy her flowers. Loving a man/woman is the greatest thing in the world.*

- *Having mutual respect, just caring for each other, you know, whatever you feel strongly about, it's love.*

- *Love is a feeling, an emotional attraction toward someone or something, knowing that you could not live without it. It is something that makes you very happy, obviously. Something you genuinely appreciate, no matter what.*

- *Love is unconditional. There are no boundaries.*

- *Eternal happiness.*

- *Love is the main thing that unites us as a human race.*

- *Love is the capacity to care for someone at a deeper level beyond yourself. It is being able to put someone before yourself and do it without thinking about it. It just comes naturally.*

Every statement is true!

Here, I would like to elaborate on the idea that love is an investment of feeling, time, effort, and money. I call this the **love input**. How can you tell whether someone is worth your investment? Do I look like a good investment to him? How can I interest him in investing in me? Now, I have the answer to why my ex left me (or, in other words, discontinued investing his time and effort in me): he simply did not see an ideal return on his investment. As blunt as this sounds, this rational understanding helped me let go and move on.

As a matter of fact, the power of love is much stronger than pure logic. Loving someone can be beyond comprehension—the reason why you love someone cannot always be explained.

Giving love involves generosity, and receiving love in return is incredibly precious.

Being loved is a fortune.

Years ago, I wrote a song called "Zero-Sum Game," in which I incorporated my knowledge of economics and finance into the lyrics. It sounds funny, but I believe that it reflects real life!

Zero-Sum Game

I took my guts and put in my faith
Made a deal I was really brave
You got me in, showed me your game
Made me believe in your angel face

You know, there's fluctuation
Between the actual and the expectation
Not that I wish, not that I hope
So cruel the reality shows

Now I woke up and cleaned up my face
Nice surprise to me, oh my babe

Get it ready, get it started
Have some fun that you set this flame

Make it nice, try to make it great
Paid my price, let me keep it safe
How we played it, how we behaved
Now it ended, baby you got me blamed

*See how much I've lost in you
*The investment in you, the effort I have put in you
*All gone in vain, all gone in plain
*See how much I've lost in you
*The capital, the time
*The wealth and the treasury
*All gone into your account
*Without a penny left for me
*Not even a piece of you.

51. Love Is an Investment

Let's perceive love from a financial point of view. In financial statements, there is a provision for impairment (also devaluation) of the assets, both tangible and intangible. A romantic relationship works in a similar way. The *love input* is a type of investment: its worth may vary, just like the price of a publicly traded stock, which fluctuates continuously. This variation may sometimes work in your favor and you will be richly rewarded. However, **passion may fade; affection may wane; a heart may change.** Therefore, keep in mind that the permanence of a relationship is not guaranteed. Always be prepared for the possibility that the return on your love input may diminish.

Love is an investment, so let's consider the following:

A. Input & Output

Just as you would be prudent when making a financial investment, you should also be careful when investing in love.

How can you maximize the return on your love input? Treat your relationship as your most valuable asset, which requires maintenance and management. In fact, your relationship should also be respected as a living being that deserves attention, effort, and care.

B. Seeding & Harvesting

How can I fill my relationship with vibrancy? Here are critical nutrients I should supply:

- A friendly personality, which keeps the atmosphere pleasant

- Reliability, which assures sustainability

- Curiosity, which adds flavor, energy, and sparkle to life

Nurture your relationship and watch it blossom!

C. Risk & Reward

A committed relationship differs from a temporary attraction. It requires ongoing effort. The right relationship will be worth your devotion.

The risks and rewards of your relationship should be considered from a long-term point of view.

What are you risking? In a financial investment, only money or other types of property are put at risk. With respect to a love partnership, you risk much more than monetary assets—you venture with your time, emotional wellness, and health, which are all priceless. So, how can you afford to be reckless when developing an intimate bond with someone you have fallen for?

From the angle of investment (please allow me to be candid), love should NOT be *unconditional*. Having learned from my education and life experience, I believe that **all kinds of love should be *conditional*, reasonably—equality, fairness, and balance form the foundation of love.** A romantic relationship is like a business deal—both parties must contribute equally according to their rights and obligations so that their relationship can last and stay healthy.

A romantic relationship is an investment, which is an asset. If it is unfortunately rotten and irremediable, it will no longer generate any benefit—it becomes a *sunk cost*, which is discussed in Chapter II (Reborn).

Do not be discouraged! Understanding the risk of falling in love will not harm your pursuit of a healthy relationship. In fact, it will secure your emotional wellness.

Unlike a failed financial investment, there is never a net loss in love. Even an unsuccessful relationship will benefit you with experience and wisdom. A lesson in reviving your heart can still be deemed a profit. Be brave enough to love if you believe that it will be rewarding.

If you invest in love wisely, you will reap the greatest fortune that life has to offer. Be confident!

*Your thoughts:

---

52. <u>Do I Regret It?</u>

If you ask me, "Do you have regrets?"

I will definitely answer, "No!"

As long as it is honest and legal, I think it is best not to repent for anything you have done.

I may have tried something that did not work. I may have adored someone who did not care for me in the same way. It is all about the experiences I have gained and the lessons I have learned. No one knows whether something will work out until he/she tries.

A fabulous friend of mine who is in her seventies once told me, "Date anyone you want. Go out with him if he is an honest person. Even if it doesn't work, you will at least learn something."

After terminating an invalid romance, the best I can do is live a better life. I believe that destiny will be kind to me and will arrange for me to meet someone more suitable in the next chapter of my life. All I need to do is turn to the next page with my courage.

As for break-ups, my friend told me that an ugly one is better than a peaceful one, because you will not miss your ex after a nasty split. I have to agree. However, to retain my decency, I broke up with my ex civilly. The fact that we never fought was what caused me to go through such hardship—the feeling of missing him made me sick.

If I cannot change something in reality, all I can do is adapt myself to it and survive as "the fittest."

Regret is probably the most ineffective course of action, whereas reviewing the past in a sensible way can be a healthy approach. Occasionally, I look at the past from my present standpoint to analyze those challenging situations and their consequences in hindsight. It is a beneficial process for me to identify what I did wrong. Then, my mistakes enlighten me, keeping me alert and cautious.

Admitting my faults takes effort, but it is worth it.

I have flaws and weaknesses and I should take action to minimize them. As the old maxim goes, *practice makes perfect.*

53. No Need to Complain About His Mother

The relationship between a woman and her man's mother is often a puzzle. My friends have complained to me from time to time about their tribulations with their mothers-in-law. It is quite a mystery why a woman and her mother-in-law sometimes cannot easily communicate.

Not long ago, I had a conversation with one of my best friends, Julie, who married the man she loves but is displeased with her mother-in-law being tough on her.

Julie grew up in a middle-class family, received higher education, performed well in school, and is now financially independent. She has been sweet and caring to her husband.

Julie: Today, I got so upset after talking to my mother-in-law. She thinks that her son is an amazing man but got married too early (in his early thirties). She wanted him to make greater achievements in his career before getting married. She said that I was so lucky, implying that I was not good enough for her son. It is unfair to me. He is also lucky to have married me.

Me: Wow, that's really hurtful. I can totally understand your frustration. To avoid making the situation worse, just try to stay calm. Also, it would be smart NOT to confront your mother-in-law because the conflict between you two will just endanger the relationship and put your husband in a difficult position. Just swallow your pride and be nice to her—smile. At least pretend to be agreeable.

Show her that you're an invaluable woman who has built a happy life together with her son. You have a great personality; you take care of her grandchild and son very well; you're financially independent, which allows your husband to stay focused on his career. Gradually, your mother-in-law will realize how fortunate her son is to have you. Besides, every mother thinks that her son is an exceptional man. You have a high IQ and now it's time to test your EQ!

Julie: My husband takes care of our baby too, and he likes it. I'm glad that he enjoys the participation. Nowadays, it's very common that men share the housework and help with parenting. However, my mother-in-law is very traditional. Her husband did not do any housework and only focused on his career. Comparing her son to her husband, she is unhappy that her son is doing "too much" for his wife—me, but it's actually for our family. She even told him not to accompany me in the delivery room when I gave birth to our son.

Me: It's such a big gap in mentality. No matter how your mother-in-law views it, if you manage the family very well, she will have nothing to criticize. I believe that one day she will change her mind if she continues to see what a wonderful family you have created together. It just takes time. You don't spend your husband's money. That's one of the reasons why he respects and loves you so much—this is what really matters.

Julie: I never took money from him or his family, not even for our wedding. My parents don't care about money. If I am happy, so are they. Thus, they have been very sweet to my husband. But look at how my mother-in-law treats me. My parents would be really disappointed and upset if they heard the hurtful words she said to me. I cry every time I think about this.

Me: Right. Money and gifts ... these material things do not count for much. It's how a couple forms a strong team that matters. I understand that this is unjust to you. I can feel your pain. If you want to cry, just go ahead and release it for a while. I weep by myself sometimes when I am treated unfairly.

Julie: I feel bad for my parents. Why does their daughter have to suffer this injustice when she doesn't deserve it?

Me: It won't be a problem if you don't view it as one. Your parents care about you, so your happiness means the most to them. Your husband loves you and that's all that matters. Talk to me, or other friends, when you feel sad. Confide in those you trust. Don't keep it to yourself. Invest some time in improving the relationship with your mother-in-law. Maybe hang out with her or even go on a trip. Make her happy, and then, when she's in a pleasant mood, talk openly to her.

Julie: Her attitude and words bother me so much.

Me: Just try to look on the bright side. You and your husband have a lovely marriage—all that one could wish for.

Julie: I'm glad that you don't need to deal with a person like this.

Me: Well, my emotional crisis was brought on by the man, not his mother. **Now that we've broken up, I don't even have the chance to suffer from the relationship with his mother.**

Julie: You don't need to waste your time with a fickle-hearted guy.

Me: Just be grateful for what you have. Don't let anything minor take your happiness away.

So, ladies and gentlemen, if you are already in a relationship with the one you love, please do not waste your valuable time being upset about his/her mother, father, siblings, relatives, friends, co-workers, pets, etc., because if he/she leaves you for someone else, you will not even have the chance to endure any issue with any of his/her associates. Appreciate your life with your loved one and just accept everything that comes with him/her. There is always a way to mediate.

In contrast, if your loved one has walked out of your life and left your heart broken in pieces, OK. Great! Live your life with relief! Now, you no longer need to struggle with any trouble affiliated with that person. Restart your era with a clean slate. You can reinstall your heart and move on with carefree joy!

Chapter XII Empowering Myself

54. Admitting My Weakness

Everything happens for a reason. So, if my ex did not choose me for a long-term romantic partnership, there must have been an explanation—it could have been that I was not good enough, or I was just not "the one."

I do not blame anyone for leaving me. Instead, the first thing I should do is acknowledge both my strengths and weaknesses objectively. I should appreciate myself for my qualities and figure out how to mitigate my deficits.

No one can be perfect, but I can keep getting closer and closer to my best self through my efforts. There is always room for me to improve. I cannot surpass everyone, but I can exceed the person I was yesterday.

When I see my self-enhancement, either when I master a new skill or become more proficient at an existing skill, I gain confidence in myself. Then, I bolster my morale to overcome the setbacks in my life. The power inside me has been ignited. I will not be taken down because of one man leaving me. I will not be forever oppressed by this cruel reality. I recognize my weaknesses and then advance myself, just as a programmer identifies technical bugs in a software program, fixes them, and then releases an upgraded version.

55. <u>Standing Up for Myself</u>

Are you a "Yes" person? Do you feel tired?

Are you a "No" person? Do you feel lonely?

If you are a "Yes" person, you often say yes to people. Consequently, people around you often ask for your help. You have earned a lot of brownie points and they love you. However, sometimes you may find yourself spending too much time on other people's matters that distract you.

If you are a "No" person, you probably often say no to people or refuse to help. Therefore, people around you keep their distance and may not care much about you. Sometimes you feel lonely, as people seem so far away.

I was somewhat of a "Yes" person before this break-up. From this perished relationship, I learned that I should stand up for myself to avoid being taken advantage of too much. Before, I offered a lot to the people around me because I enjoyed being appreciated. This break-up was a wake-up call for me. I realized that many of the things I had done for my ex, as well as for others, were actually unnecessary, or went unreciprocated. I felt tired, physically and mentally.

I have learned that there should be balance between *yes* and *no*. It is very kind of you to say yes and offer help to a reasonable extent within your capability. However, if this offer goes too far or even starts to be harmful to you, think twice! Consider saying no when you feel that someone might be taking advantage of you. Stop what starts to make you feel uncomfortable.

This is what I want you to know:

Stand up for yourself!

Balance in a relationship is based on equality. If the situation becomes unfair, be brave and speak up!

56. Dealing with Difficult People Around Me

I am not a negative person myself, but I cannot stop the negativity brought on by the people around me.

For example, my mother is a great person, but she has her flaw: a short temper. If someone or something goes against her wishes, she will easily get irritated. If someone continues to confront her when she is already upset, she will become aggravated and let hurtful words loose. We have a close relationship, but once in a while I have to handle this difficult part of her personality. Every time, I simply compromised with her because an argument would not help while she was angry. Then, in the next few days, she would tell me that she should not have yelled at me and did not remember what she had actually said.

Besides my mom, I have had to face many other difficult people in my life. Some have been pessimistic and frequently complained, some moody and quick to lose their temper, and some critical and difficult to please. They have emerged throughout my life in an endless stream.

I once worked in a team of five people on a project. One of my team members said to herself many times a day, "I am really struggling with this!" Maybe she felt better after expressing her feelings, or she did not realize that she was doing so. I would not want to have her on my team again because her uneasiness had an adverse impact on others.

Here I would like to point out:

1. Difficult people and their negativity are unavoidable in life. If I cannot get away from them, I have to learn to deal with them.

2. I do not want to be the kind of person who has an unfavorable influence on others, so I try to avoid picking up the behaviors I dislike.

Dealing with an irritable person requires effort and cleverness. From my experience, the best way to cope with an intense situation with such a person is to pause or reasonably compromise at that moment, and then, when that person has calmed down, try to converse with him/her again. This is the time to utilize one's EQ. As I observe, people with a higher EQ tend to be more successful in life.

Why should I compromise with an angry person? Here are some examples of why some people easily get mad and my responses to the situations:

Reason	My Response
Lack of confidence: They are not able to convince people by giving substantial reasons, so they can only make people agree by force.	Understand their intentions and negotiate in a flexible and clever way.
Stress: They are under pressure as they are already threatened by their own difficult situations.	Offer them compassion and dissolve the conflicts amicably and sagaciously.
Lack of self-discipline: They are not good at controlling their temper.	Accept who they are, as you cannot easily change them. Self-discipline cannot be formed overnight.
Disrespectful toward others: They are used to having people obey them, so they are not used to taking others' advice or listening to others' opinions.	There is no point in reasoning with people who behave this way. Stay calm during the communication. If it is too much for you, find a polite way to keep a reasonable distance from them.

167

To handle difficult people and their issues requires ingenuity, which can be cultivated through the continuous practice of communication and interpersonal skills. Putting yourself in other people's shoes is the first step.

57. One Goal at a Time

Just as a car needs gas to be driven, we need energy to propel our lives forward. What is the energy source? I believe that one's satisfaction from his/her achievements is the biggest motivation in life.

How do you attain all of your goals? You have small, medium, and large plans throughout your life. Focus on one at a time and eventually you will accomplish them all. If you exert yourself and try to complete them all at once, you may end up with nothing significant.

Think about the path to your destination carefully. Then, concentrate!

Focus will foster efficiency. Multitasking is challenging and it needs strong skills in time management. Some time ago, I tried for a year to carry out many projects to build a new career for myself: songwriting, scriptwriting, video distribution, testing for the certified public accountant (CPA) license, and pursuing funding for my start-up company. My time became fragmented, handling many different tasks every day. I was overwhelmed for the entire year, and sadly ended up with no major mission accomplished.

Drawing from my lessons, this is what I suggest:

Identify your short-term and long-term goals, and then make things happen one by one.

This does not imply that you cannot achieve all of them. It means that setting a reasonable schedule to fulfill your ambitions step by step can lead to greater efficiency. Preparing your agenda (and adjusting throughout the whole process) is the first critical step. By accomplishing one substantial task, you gain confidence. Starting from one small victory, you are working at your best capacity and you will eventually actualize your dreams in the quickest way!

In my own experience, I wrote half of this book in just three months following my break-up, as I made use of the situation.

All along, I had been longing to write several books with intriguing stories by the time I reached the age of sixty, or when I became financially flexible with a lot of spare time. Yet, I did not have the chance to start writing any scripts as I had been fully devoting myself to my career in the field of finance and then to a start-up business.

All of a sudden, this unfortunate break-up befell me. I was utterly overwhelmed for at least three months. I worried that I was going to be paralyzed from sleep deprivation, so I tried my best to record the emotional hurricane inside my head. It was like a spark that lit a fire within me. Thoughts kept popping up in my mind. I spent most of my time after work writing this book instead of going out to date or enjoying other leisure activities. Whenever an idea flashed through my mind, I immediately jotted down the outline and then elaborated upon it when I had sufficient free time on weekends. From a few paragraphs about my heartbreak, I documented my entire perception of surmounting an emotional crisis. Eventually, I completed this book in a year and a half.

I would never have expected to write a book while working on a start-up business, which was already consuming the majority of my energy. Surprisingly, I did it, by properly allocating my time and concentration. When I hold a copy of this book, I feel spectacular—how satisfying it is!

Therefore, I am sure that you can also make the most of your time and create something fulfilling and rewarding!

Focus is vital in time management. Meanwhile, work-life balance is the basis of sustainability. So, it is best for one to reasonably apportion his/her time between work and rest. Effective relaxation includes listening to music, singing, dancing, exercising, playing sports, going to parties and festivals, shopping, browsing social media, watching movies, reading, writing, cooking, painting, crafting, gardening—anything and everything you find enjoyable!

More about time management is discussed in Section 77 (As Time Goes By) and Section 78 (How Efficient Are My 24 Hours?) of Chapter XIV (How Much These Types of Value Mean to Me).

Think about what deserves your attention now. When you have a solid goal, stay focused!

*What deserves your focus now?

----

58. <u>Purifying My Mind</u>

My mind needs a detox from time to time, just like my body.

Due to the depression arising from my break-up, unsuccessful business deals, and financial difficulties, my mind was a MESS!

On the outside, I looked fine, but my mind was a MESS!

My room was neat and tidy, but my mind was a total MESS!

The first thing I needed to do was reorganize my mind.

My soul is like a huge mansion. For this grand building, I first need a concrete foundation to support the whole structure. The foundation of my soul is my belief in myself. Despite the rain and thunder in life, I should remain steadfast with faith in myself. All the challenges in front of me are just temporary, NOT permanent. The perfect storm will certainly be over tomorrow.

While being oppressed by my emotional disaster, I took some time to contemplate. What went wrong after all? I listed all my problems and then analyzed them—which of my difficulties could be solved quickly and which needed more of my time? After assessing my situation objectively, I made a new plan for myself and stuck to it.

I learned to let go. I tried to replace my distressing memories with something new by proactively visiting new places, checking out new products, meeting new people, and practicing new skills. **A dynamic life revived me!**

Just be courageous enough to accept new things. Broaden your vision. Embrace a fresh breeze!

Abandon unnecessary demands!

Why am I unhappy? Because I do not get what I want. So, if I desire less, I will be able to enjoy more.

When my mind is crammed with needs, my head, the control panel of my entire body, cannot function properly. I should slow down and smell the flowers to refresh my brain.

Five things that can calm me down may work for you too:

1. Music: listening to guitar, piano, violin, and other musical instruments is very pleasant. Singing along is even more delightful. Music "massages" my nerves.
2. Fitness exercise: jumping, dancing, and sweating relax my body. Also, these activities accelerate my blood flow, enabling nutrients to be delivered to my brain.
3. Visiting a new place: new scenes and faces amaze me. Smelling new scents makes me feel so revitalized.
4. Pets: the most consoling time for me was when I bathed my dog, Shanelle, while she was alive. When a cute animal shows me affection, my heart melts!
5. Cooking: it blocks out the chaos in my mind as it requires my attention to avoid burning the food. In addition, making something delicious and wholesome is an immense joy!

After cooling down my mind, I sort out the different voices in my heart. Now, there are options in front of me and I am hesitating at the crossroad of choices. I should listen to my heart and appeal to my sanity to decide on my direction.

After reorganizing my thoughts, I tidy up my belongings. As soon as the superfluous stuff in my living and working environments is cleared, I feel relieved. The ideas in my mind and the items in my sight are in order once again.

Five tips to help organize your belongings:

1. Go through everything: get a big trash bin ready to discard useless things. Look over everything and think about the scenarios in which these items can be used.
2. Get rid of obsolete things, such as those expired, dried out, or broken. If you want to store something vintage or memorable, save it in an "antique box."
3. Group things of the same type. Prepare some organizers and shelves in advance.
4. Gather things in order: from the most to the least used, from high to low in value, from big to small, from long to short, etc.
5. Get something new: write down a list of things for replacement.

The moment I throw that box of trash into the garbage container, I feel entirely refreshed. It is an official goodbye to the past!

Purifying my mind is an ongoing practice. At the end of the day, I review what I have accomplished and reset my mind for tomorrow.

*List your approaches to clearing your mind:

----

59. Growing Affection for Myself

People say, "You must love yourself before you can love others."

Here, I would like to discuss *self-admiration* in a positive and healthy way, not as anything negative associated with narcissism. Everyone should admire themselves at a reasonable level. Everyone possesses his/her unique qualities and charms. There must be a way for one to discover his/her own worth.

On the basis of my self-affection, I follow my discipline to "optimize" myself. Beyond merely breathing, eating, defecating, and sleeping every day, I desire to elevate my life to a higher level. I make time and effort to create something cool to satisfy myself. Additionally, I am heartened when I earn people's appreciation.

From a young age, I have loved looking at myself in the mirror, making different funny faces. I am enchanted by my eyes, lips, cheeks, etc. When I was a child, I wondered how my eyes were able to blink and roll. As I got older, I started to have dark circles under my eyes and wrinkles on my skin. I wondered how they had been formed. I noticed changes in my body as time went by. Sometimes I look good and sometimes not so much. Besides being gratified by my poise, I am able to think and act of my own accord. I am capable of creating value for myself through years of study, work, and life experience. I can turn my prosaic days into delectable moments. I know that I am not perfect, but I am happy just being who I am. I guess I am a little bit obsessed with myself, in a cute and harmless sort of way.

My rationale is:

If I cannot find a reason to be fond of myself, how can I convince others to appreciate me?

Nature on this planet is astonishing. As an advanced creature, a human being is incredibly miraculous. I am integrated into this awe-inspiring world—isn't it fascinating?

There is no way I cannot love myself. Especially while undergoing an emotional tsunami, I need to hold onto the trust that I possess my own value!

Developing affection for myself is a beautiful matter.

*List what you like about yourself (be confident):

----

60. <u>Appreciating Life as a Miracle</u>

This world is a miracle. Do you know how many planets there are in the universe? Innumerable. Do you know how many planets there are like Earth? So far, I know of only this one.

Being a living creature in this world is a precious opportunity. Being born as a human being with an independent mind is as lucky as winning the lottery! Do you know how many people have been killed by accidents, disease, and wars? Sadly, too many to count.

Survival is already a miracle.

From a fertilized egg inside my mother's womb to a grown-up person, I am literally a marvel—I was actually a swimming champion at the very beginning of my journey (as you know, the winning sperm fertilizes the egg)! I am grateful for the fact that I am still breathing and enjoying my presence on this splendid planet. I should not let anything break me down! Never again! Certainly not a bloody stupid break-up!

*List your plan to keep your life dynamic:

Chapter XIII Life Is a Process

61. <u>All Aboard! This Is a Nonstop Journey!</u>

After each of my break-ups, I confided in a friend who is in her seventies and filled with wisdom. This is what she told me every time:

There is always another bus.

If you have missed it, it is already gone. It did not wait for you, so just accept that fact. Another bus will arrive in ten minutes or so. Just be a bit patient. It will take you to your destination and offer you magnificent views along the way!

Another friend told me that, during your lifetime exploration, a man gets on the same bus and stays with you for a period of time, and then gets off at some point. If he does not leave, there will be no seat for someone new. Let him go. Let someone new come to join your tour.

A lot of my efforts of trying may be in vain, but **life is a one-way nonstop journey**, and there is no point in staying stranded in the past, feeling dispirited. My experiment of romance at least has satisfied my curiosity about being human.

It could be disheartening that I had been spinning, searching, and bustling around, but eventually, I realized that I was back to the starting point, as if nothing had happened. All I obtained was a chain of memories.

Have I gained anything from my futile attempts? I believe that my tracks pave the way to my destination. Whether my endeavors have turned out to be successful or not, they have become footprints in my lifetime voyage.

The bitterness of my failures makes my achievements taste even better.

62. Discovering a New Land

Fighting against the break-up trauma, I came to understand that I should not be dejected that there was nowhere in that old land in which my heart belonged. Instead, I should appreciate the opportunity that I have been forced to discover a new territory!

Life is precious. If I tie my ship to one small port, I may just miss out on the whole spectacular continent.

The story of Columbus discovering America has greatly inspired me. Regardless of the enormous risk, he sailed across oceans to explore. Nothing was guaranteed. He was driven by his ambition to navigate toward the far, unknown, and endless landscape.

My love life is just the same. Since that old land has turned sour, I must summon up the courage to set off from this old port and embark on another expedition!

One day when I discover a new companion for a romantic adventure, my love life will launch a brand-new series.

One time, I was sitting on some rocks at a wide beach, alone, letting the rough, cold tide run over my feet. The sea was roaring; the wind was raging. No one else was around me. At that moment, I was impressed by how immense and strong nature was. In comparison, my sorrows and struggles seemed so insignificant.

I am just one tiny little creature in this gigantic world, in awe of nature. I cannot change it, so I adapt myself to it.

63. **Dating at Different Depths**

In my career, I have been trained to perform business analyses and conclude them with a summary. While pondering over love matters, I have used the same skills to categorize dating situations at different levels from what I have seen and heard in today's society.

I believe that when I am fostering a romance with a man, my understanding of our dating status should be equivalent to his. If there is a gap between our expectations for each other, at least one of us will likely end up getting hurt at some point.

Here are my observations with respect to dating at different depths (there is no intent for judgment here and you may just laugh):

- Hooking up:

   A so-called "one-night stand" or fleeting romance that allows two people to enjoy the moment without any pressure of a future relationship. It is almost like a dessert which is able to temporarily satisfy one's appetite.

- Friends with benefits:

   Have you seen the movie with this title? It is actually a sweet love story. In real life, this term refers to two people who are friends with the added mutual benefit of sex without strings to bind these two partners. Personally, I believe that a continuous sexual relationship involves affection, whether one is aware of it or not. If sex can be completely separated from emotion, I doubt whether that sex can be amazing ... I bet that at least one party will eventually end up getting his/her feelings hurt.

- Casual dating:

  Two people enjoy each other's company whenever they want to get together to have a taste of romance, or even lust, without being held back by the mutual requirement of commitment or exclusivity. This is similar to experimenting before moving on to a committed relationship.

- Open/non-exclusive relationship:

  Two lovers toy with the idea of being a couple while being open to trying multiple romantic experiences at the same time. They allow each other to date other people. In other words, it is like sampling different flavors of ice cream before finally deciding on one to purchase.

  The first time I heard the term "open relationship" is an interesting story: I was in San Francisco for a week-long visit, during which I met a charming young man on a train who was also in town for a short business trip. We became acquainted, and the next day, we attended a public event together. Later, we went to dinner and had a joyful time. Afterward, while walking to a taxi line at the end of the night, he suddenly stopped me and held me in his arms. Then, we had the following dialogue:

  Him: Do you want to have sex with me?

  Me: Um ... do you have a girlfriend?

  He did not answer right away. We froze for a moment, and then we moved forward on the street.

  After walking for a while, he responded: Yes, but we're in an open relationship.

Me: No! I'm going home now. Thanks for your company this evening.

Him: Why?

Me: I don't want her to hate me.

Him: She won't hate you, because if we were to have sex, I would tell her.

Me: What???!!! (My eyes opened wide.)

I jumped into a taxi right away and left.

In fact, I was grateful for his honesty. I wondered, if he had asked another woman, she might not have had such a problem with it. Having grown up in a traditional society myself, I did not want to get involved in this type of affair.

- Exclusive relationship:

  Finally, after leaping over all the obstacles, two people commit to each other for a serious relationship, which entitles the lovebirds to each other's loyalty.

No judgment on any dating status outlined above is implied here. People make their own choices and craft their own lifestyles. This just reflects the fact that it can be a long process to find one's perfect mate.

*Do you have any funny dating stories that can make you laugh in hindsight?

----

64. If I Could Turn Back Time

During the period I was trapped in the swamp of my heartbreak, I could not help but regret the silly things I had done for my ex. Remorse is a sad thing. Can I turn back time and redo something? Of course, I cannot.

The truth is, even if I went back in time to redo it all, the chance that I could get a much better outcome today is low, because my capability yesterday was already developed to the maximum with my best efforts at that time. That means, another approach would not make a major difference. Thus, I should not linger in the recollections. I just need to accept what happened and look ahead. On the other hand, I can definitely fortify myself from now on and tighten my grip on my future.

The two most discouraging sentences are: "I should have done ..." and "I shouldn't have done ..."

I hate regretting what I have done in the past. What is done is already done. I should not look back. I should look forward. "I am going to do ..." sounds much more constructive!

Take control of today. Plan for tomorrow. Make sure that the "me" of tomorrow will not regret what I do today.

Similar to the butterfly effect, a small change today may lead to a huge difference tomorrow.

Everything restarts from now!

Regardless of anything that happened in the past, I assume that my destiny commences as of this morning. There have been times when I achieved nothing, as well as times when I gained a lot and then lost it all. **The past vanishes along with time.** From the moment I see the sunrise, I am the master of today.

65. "After I Die, the Carpet Is Still There."

Here is a humorous anecdote about letting go of unimportant things in life:

On one occasion, I stayed at my friend's apartment for a few months and lived happily with her and her dog, Mr. Mocha, with the exception of one funny drama. Mocha once peed on a large carpet in my room. I informed my friend of the mess and she cleaned the spot right away. A few weeks later, I found another urine stain that had altered the color of the carpet in that area. This was our conversation when I told her about Mocha's second instance of misbehavior on the carpet:

Her: Why didn't you tell me right after Mocha peed? Now the stain cannot be removed. This is one of my favorite carpets.

Me: I noticed only one spot, and I told you last time. If I had known there was another spot, I would have told you immediately.

She was unhappy because she liked the carpet a lot.

Her (after a sigh): That's all right. Let it be. I don't care about the stain anymore. After I die, the carpet will still be there.

Me: Yeah! After we all die, your carpet will still be here.

We giggled.

After I die, the carpet will remain. Isn't it true? Sometimes we become so fixated on some material objects and we may forget that after our lives end, only those tangible things will continue to exist.

Since gaining an understanding of the tremendous value of being alive, I am no longer easily upset by trivial matters. My vivacious life means much more to me than anything external.

66. A Letter to My Future Self 10 Years from Now

Dear Self of 2030 (ten years from now):

First off, I hope that you are still living in this world.

Secondly, I hope that you are proud of me, your past, and all that you have done.

You must be really excited reading this letter.

Answer my questions first:

1. How is my book, *Break-Up Survival*, doing? Have you made it into a movie yet?

2. Are you living happily with a man now? I know you are picky, but since you are independent, there is nothing wrong with being prudent.

3. Is there still a chance that your ex will come back to you? He seriously broke my heart. You remember, don't you? I hope that you have already forgotten the pain, though I did write the song "Remember Me."

4. Is there anything you regret? Well, I have done my best.

5. Are you living the life I set out to have? Do you have time to do what you are enthusiastic about?

6. Have you made a zombie-apocalypse movie yet? That has been our life goal!

7. Have you created the "Free Trade Charity Platform" where people can donate services, products, and cash? You and I planned to do this when we were financially established and had plenty of free time. It would be a benevolent project.

8. Are you physically healthy? In case you are not, do not be too harsh on yourself.

9. Are you emotionally stronger? If, by any chance, you are confronted with another emotional crisis, please do not blame yourself. Be lenient with yourself when it comes to the

puzzling subject of LOVE. You are made of warm flesh and blood, and this is a human thing.

10. Time did not change you, did it?

You and I desire to live as long as possible, so we are very vigilant and mindful at all times. I think you are not yet ready to try anything extreme, such as skydiving and bungee jumping ... maybe until thirty years from now when we have accomplished everything we aspire to. Do not be naughty!

It is a fair guess to say that the world should be incredibly advanced and modern. Are there plenty of robots on the street? In case your world is crueler and harsher, remember, you always think independently with your sagacity.

I hope that by now, you have at least one child and one dog. I know you are very caring, but do not forget to take care of yourself.

There must have been a lot of ups and downs in your life and career over the past ten years. You have probably learned a lot from different dilemmas and predicaments. Do not let people's words bother you. **I believe that you have collected more wisdom than age throughout these years.**

Be brave to pursue love on the premise of physical wellness. I am sure that since having survived this break-up, you must be unbreakable.

Nothing can defeat you.

Please write another letter to your 10-Years-From-Now Self, and see what questions you have this time.

Love yourself above all else!

Sincerely yours,

Me in 2020.

67. You Deserve a Rest

Have you been exerting yourself on an upward climb throughout your entire life? You deserve to have a rest. Just find a reason to take a break and recharge yourself. If your phone's battery is running low and it is going to shut down, it needs to be charged. So do you!

"Overdrawing" your energy is not a smart strategy. I have learned many lessons from overusing my body, which caused me to lose much more than I gained. This is my sincere advice to you:

Do not overrun yourself too often!

Sometimes you feel exhausted from striving in life: for a career, an academic degree, power, or a relationship. You may question yourself: Am I working this hard just to wear myself out?

When your goal is high, the path is laborious, because you are continually climbing. To ascend uphill, you need to overcome gravity, unlike going downhill, when gravity assists you. It takes your willpower and persistence. Yet, your body is neither replaceable nor made of stainless steel. If you are serious about your goal, plan for the long run. Recess when necessary, and then continue with a robust body!

Once in a while, fleeing from your tedious world can be beneficial. Your purely independent getaway can be a day when you are alone, at a place where no one knows you, so that you are able to embrace carefree joy. That feeling is special and fantastic.

The gratification from the day may not be the feeling of satisfaction from how much money you have made. It can be the pleasure you feel while enjoying a cup of tea peacefully, recalling the little things that make you feel alive. It can also be a sentimental moment while listening to a song that resonates with you and touches your heart.

Chapter XIV   How Much These Types of Value Mean to Me

Value of Judgment

68.   Computing the Fair Value

I would like to draw your attention to a financial term: **fair value**. In addition to its original meaning, a number for accounting purposes, I have found this concept very helpful in forming my perspective throughout my life.

Fair value technically refers to the reasonable worth of an item on the open market. The definition and introduction of fair value can be easily found on the Internet. For example, according to Investopedia, "In investing, fair value refers to an asset's sale price agreed upon by a willing buyer and seller, assuming both parties are knowledgeable and enter the transaction freely. In accounting, fair value represents the estimated worth of various assets and liabilities that must be listed on a company's books." (updated May 16, 2019).

With this concept in mind, in daily life, I try to measure matters and things around me by considering their fair value, so that I can make the best decisions after weighing up the costs and benefits. The fair value of an act (by my personal calculation) is:

How much it will enable me to grow.

For example, if I attain a specific academic degree, I will be eligible for a rewarding career, which will allow me to lead a quality life and be part of an elite network of professionals. Therefore, the fair value of this academic degree is evaluated not only by the salary it generates, but also by how much it can advance my reputation and life overall. The total benefit includes the earnings, intangible assets (knowledge, logical thinking, experience, professional network, etc.), and opportunities that come along with the degree. Perceiving it as a package deal, the value can be inestimable.

The same theory applies to my break-up, which has propelled me to unveil a new vision of myself. It motivated me to reassess the worth of my life and write this book (which has a particular value of its own), aiming to benefit my readers.

How much did this break-up help me grow? So much that it is immeasurable!

Fair value is an index, indicating how worthy an opportunity or an object is to me. Fair value is comprised of not only the price as it presents now, but also the long-term intrinsic value.

Everything that has happened to me, including an actualized wish, a failed attempt, and an effort in my pursuit of happiness, carries a value.

Life is like a game. There may not be any winners or losers, but everyone is a participant.

Play the game in the way that is most comfortable for you. Remember that there is always something to be gained from a failure or loss. It is OK to incur a loss as long as you never lose hope.

Sometimes the value of a failure exceeds that of a success, because a failure results in your remarkable growth. With an optimistic attitude, you will collect a notable reward that accrues from failing and losing.

*List the things and matters that have the highest value for you currently:

----

69. The Invisible Rating Cast on Me

I believe that I have been assessed (or judged, if you allow me to express boldly) by others throughout my life, based on how much my unique value means to them in different situations. This value is what makes people want to **spend time with**, **date**, **hire**, or **partner with me**. My rating is given according to the merit that I bring to the table for my team.

This invisible rating by society is just like the grade-point average (GPA) I earned at school after I studied for the whole semester and concluded it with a final test.

My worth varies for different people in different scenarios. These counterparts can be my family, school, company, team, business partners, friends, or lover. They solicit my contributions in different ways.

In a romantic relationship, my partner's consideration regarding my invisible rating consists of (in brief, what he wants from me):

- Manner
- Intelligence
- Personality
- Wealth

This is similar to what I described in the Four Dimensions in Section 27 (Envisioning My Future Mate).

In this diversified society, people tend to get along with the individuals who are compatible with them—they are similar in lifestyle, interests, and characteristics.

Thus, if I want to find someone with great competence (for example: appealing, smart, kind, and capable of developing his career) for a romantic partnership, it means I am asking for a high rating. At this point, I should first assess myself—what is the range of my rating? Reviewing my unsuccessful relationship, knowing that my score in terms of life status was much lower than my ex's, I should be able to understand why he left me. If someone merely finds me special looks-wise, he may be happy to have a fling with me. However, he may not tend to establish a substantial relationship. In short, he may play with me, but not stay with me.

This resembles attending an interview for a significant position in a company. If I would like to secure a promising job with high pay, professional colleagues, a premium work environment, an excellent corporate culture, and an opportunity for career growth, I have to be qualified—possessing the capabilities required for this job, such as a license, certificates, academic proof, and various skills.

Every relationship (romantic, friendly, or professional) is ultimately a matter of matchmaking. The commitment of a relationship is like a fair trade, in which both partners contribute equally.

So, my ex did not stay with me because I could not give him what he wanted. Period.

I have to be realistic and acknowledge that what I am facing is reality, which can be cruel, not a fairy tale or a classic romantic comedy.

Now, I understand that a good match requires comparability. Instead of being deflated, I am stimulated to position myself on the same level of ability as my ideal counterpart. This is how I create an incentive to whip myself forward.

70. <u>More Money, Less Heartbreak</u>

Quite often, it seems that rich people suffer less from heartbreak, doesn't it? The reality is, rich people can find replacements more quickly. Don't you think so? This may sound blunt, but it is what I have observed.

People say, "Oh, money cannot buy happiness." This may be mostly true. Yet, I would like to point out that, although money cannot buy all kinds of happiness, it can buy time by way of saving time (for example, hiring professionals to carry out specific tasks for you to avoid hassles). With wealth, it can be easier for a person to move on from a break-up, because he/she has more time to meet new people, try new things, and develop his/her potential to regain happiness.

This perception sounds ruthless and superficial, but it spurs me to resuscitate myself after the emotional catastrophe by proactively improving the quality of my life.

So, the key is to make more honest money!

71. <u>Earning Good and Honest Money</u>

From my years of work experience, here is my understanding of how honest money is made—simple and straightforward:

- People pay for the value you render;
- The value you render means how thoroughly you solve people's problems;
- People's problems arise from:
    - Lack of time
    - Lack of skill
    - Location

So, the way you make honest money is:

You use your knowledge, skills, capabilities, or products to save people's time by solving their problems in a specific location.

For example, from my work experience of financial statement auditing as an auditor, I have learned how a company is willing to pay for a professional service:

Companies engage financial auditors (very often, CPA firms) to perform the audit procedures required by auditing standards to review and examine their financial statements independently and objectively. Auditors use their knowledge and professional skills to help companies (their clients) identify errors in their financial statements, and then propose corresponding adjustments to correct them. After completing the entire auditing process, auditors finally express an audit opinion in written form if the company's financial statements have been fairly presented to give a true and fair view of the company's operating results. This audit report provides the related users (shareholders, investors, management, authorities, and other parties concerned) with a certain level of assurance. This is the value that auditors contribute to their clients in exchange for service fees.

Another example is this book, *Break-Up Survival*. I wrote it to share my experience and perspective of surviving an emotional crisis because I hope to 1) help you recover from your heartbreak efficiently, 2) save you a great amount of time in tangling with your bitterness, and 3) inspire you to write down your ideas. If you have enjoyed and benefited from reading my thoughts, I will be truly happy knowing that my book holds some usefulness.

The money you earn equals the value you generate. This value can come from:

- **Your talent,**
- **Your skill that exceeds others',**
- **Your ability to help people save their time, or,**
- **The convenience you create for people.**

This is the worth that people are willing to pay for.

To be clear, I am not encouraging you to be a gold-digger or a greedy person. The idea is to earn an income based on honesty and integrity. The aim is to discover your potential that can be utilized to benefit others. Accordingly, you use your value to fairly reap your fortune.

As I have learned from my work across various industries, there are three critical factors to making honest money:

- **Exposure: make yourself and your product seen and heard**
- **Evidence: prove the value of yourself and your product**
- **Energy: maximize the effectiveness and efficiency of your service and product**

People are willing to trade their assets for the value you create. Honest money makes a person truly happy, so be bold and earn it!

Do not be shy. Let yourself shine!

*List your talents that may be monetized:

----

72. <u>Who Would Not Want a Wealthy Warrior?</u>

As a woman, I consulted my friends about how to win a man over without appearing desperate. Some of my girlfriends told me that men are attracted to capable women who are like warriors.

So, what makes me a warrior?

A woman who is wealthy in all of the following five ways can be a warrior:

- Financially: the woman is independent and able to create a nice life for herself;

- Physically: the woman is enchanting, elegant, and energetic;

- Mentally: the woman is wise, understands life, and can carry on meaningful conversations;

- Emotionally: the woman is warm-hearted, considerate, and compassionate; and

- Spiritually: the woman has an aura of goodness and is able to beneficially influence people around her.

Once I attain all five types of "wealth," I will be well-rounded and confident enough NOT to worry about how to "hunt a man down," because he will approach me instead. **All I need to do first is glow!**

To be a warrior, I have to fight my inner drives as well. The heartbreak has been torturing me and the only way out is to "optimize" myself. Thus, I must adhere to my self-discipline to reach my best self! What is self-discipline? I believe that self-discipline is to defy my instincts for my own good, such as:

- Naturally, I want to date a man and enjoy romance, but I cannot let myself do that now because I must focus my time on my career this year.

- Naturally, I want to have desserts and I love them, but I cannot eat that now because I am on a diet.

- Naturally, I want to relax and rest, but I cannot allow myself to be lazy. I must do exercise for an hour each day to strengthen my body.

To become a warrior takes a lot of effort, but you are ready to excel, aren't you?

73. __Dating Like a Professional__

Just as I have to be professional at my job, I should be masterful at managing my love life, too.

Through my jobs, I have learned the essential qualities required to handle my duties properly, which can also be translated into my dating life:

- Setting goals

  My goal plays the role of navigator. "What do I want from this date?" would be a good question to start with.

- Communication

  We all understand the theories of how to be a good communicator, but in practice, it is not as easy as we imagine. Thinking from the other party's point of view is the basis for effective communication. Everyone has his/her own personality. It takes time to observe and comprehend. Sometimes compromise and mediation are unavoidable.

- Technical skills

  Just as doctors, accountants, engineers, lawyers, and pilots need specialized skills to perform their tasks, a lover should know the techniques to foster a romantic bond. To be a proficient lover, I need to demonstrate my competence in cooking, cleaning, caring, and entertaining. Of course, a bit of artistic talent, such as singing, dancing, and playing musical instruments, is the icing on the cake. I should ask myself constantly: How can I ensure that my lover always gives me a five-star review?

- Adjustment for adaptation

  Unexpected situations happen all the time, and as a result, I need to modify my strategy accordingly whenever a significant matter comes up. If my lover enters into a major life transition that will also affect me, how much am I willing to adjust my life? Sometimes sacrifices need to be made for love.

- Review from time to time

  In a relationship, there are fantastic moments, but, there also may be disagreements, arguments, or fights. Or, both parties may have been tolerating each other to a certain extent, or even in a cold war. Sometimes things work out; sometimes problems worsen. There are always things to learn from successes and failures. A relationship can be strengthened by creating memorable times and resolving issues.

When I become a sophisticated dater, I will not panic about losing a loved one because my future sweetheart will come along in my life and adore me.

*Are you ready to be a "professional" dater?

----

74. <u>Opportunity Cost: The Benchmark for Decision-Making</u>

The speed of time is the only thing that is fair to everyone. We are all allotted 24 hours in a day. Some people manage their 24 hours well and establish ongoing value for the future, while others do not. The allocation of 24 hours is like making investments. I should schedule my time wisely to acquire the best return on investment.

To plan my time ideally by setting priorities, the first step is to determine the **opportunity cost**, an important consideration in economics, which can be translated into a parameter for decision-making in daily life.

Explained by James M. Buchanan, a recognized American economist, opportunity cost (also known as "alternative cost"), is "the evaluation placed on the most highly valued of the rejected alternatives or opportunities. It is that value that is given up or sacrificed in order to secure the higher value that selection of the chosen object embodies."

From my perspective, explicitly, in daily life opportunity cost is the **highest reasonable value that is given up while I choose another option that means the most to me**. For example, let's say I work as a chef in a restaurant for $50/hour. If I take a leave for a day of eight working hours in my regular working schedule to attend a class, I am waiving $400 ($50/hour x 8 hours) in income—I am willingly giving up the opportunity to earn a certain amount of income that I am capable of making. The opportunity cost of eight hours during my regular work time is $400. It means that the class I will attend by taking off from my job is worth more than $400 to me.

Opportunity cost is the most important consideration for both my daily decision-making and my long-term planning. I use it to measure my approaches to my goals. It guides me to determine what I should do and should NOT do each day.

In reality, cases of evaluating opportunity cost can be:

Related to dating:

- I spend time looking for a boyfriend as opposed to hunting for a better job or business opportunity;
- I spend time on a man to secure a relationship rather than learning something new; or
- I spend time fighting with a man, trying to solve an issue between us instead of doing something enjoyable.

Related to other activities in daily life:

- I go out with friends to learn new things rather than stay alone to write something interesting;
- I study for a profession that will secure my career rather than do something I am naturally passionate about to develop my talent;
- I stay home to relax my body and mind rather than work overtime to get a project done perfectly; or
- I watch a movie to enjoy an easy time rather than exercise.

There is no right or wrong here. Each option has its own rationale. It is just a matter of choice.

There is nothing wrong with spending time seeking a boyfriend as opposed to developing your career. Life is not all about working and making money. Your search for a man may turn out to be in vain, or you may end up discovering a lifelong partner. You will never know until you try. Life is about finding balance in its different stages and making every day satisfactory.

Here is my life experience in selecting an option:

After quitting my job as an auditor in 2012, I decided to broaden my outlook on the world through experiencing as many new things as possible. Within six months, I had spent almost all of my savings traveling—visiting tourist attractions, attending events, eating at popular restaurants, and going shopping.

Right after that, I started a new business in a new field instead of continuing my original profession. Due to the financial strain after using up my savings on traveling, I had to sell my only property to inject funding into my start-up business. Some of my friends suggested I stick to the same profession and push my career to the next level. That was thoughtful advice, but I did not take it. I understood that it was risky for me to start from scratch in an industry in which I was a newcomer. Still, in order to pursue what I am enthusiastic about, I was ready to risk all my assets and spend several years exploring a path that would allow me to build my new career for the next decade.

In terms of making a choice between various options, some things must be given up. This concept is expressed in the popular proverb *you can't have your cake and eat it, too.* Evaluating opportunity cost is a helpful and practical method one can use to make decisions, especially while arranging what to do during his/her PRIME TIME. To flourish, we should learn what and how to give up.

75. Reputation: Hard to Build, Easy to Break

It takes enormous effort to build a good reputation; yet one critical mistake can cause a person to lose it entirely. This is appalling but true!

Building and maintaining a good name is like accumulating a fortune.

From my whole life, watching other people and myself, I have learned that to build my reputation, the first thing I need to do is avoid making errors.

Reputation in relation to romantic matters holds its own importance. From my observations, some people date casually, changing partners frequently, and some even have short-term relationships with those in their circle of friends. In this case, they build quite a "network of exes" in which these active daters may ultimately come across each other by chance (well, this world is sometimes ridiculously small). For example, one's ex happens to be the ex of many other people, too. It would be such an awkward situation if these individuals and their common ex all showed up to the same event. These people's dating histories may become known by their acquaintances. Consequently, rumors may fly. Some of the affairs of the active daters could drift into others' gossip material.

Well, personally, I would not want to be the ex of someone who has a lot of exes already, consequentially causing me to become a part of his large group of former lovers. In other words, I would not want to date a well-known heartbreaker. Even if I did, I would keep it a secret. I can imagine that if I happened to be randomly assigned to sit at the same table with my ex and several of his other exes all together at a business dinner, I would feel extremely uncomfortable and be dying to run away from that situation as soon as possible (if you happen to have found yourself in this kind of circumstance, I hope my honesty has not offended you).

Vice versa, would my future partner mind whom I had dated before? I guess he would. I am afraid that he would compare me to those people my ex had openly dated. Are you laughing at my concerns now? They are ridiculous but realistic, aren't they?

If I become someone's ex, I hope that this special person has a good reputation, so that I, being simply another one of his past lovers, do not look foolish. Don't you agree?

Reputation in relation to work and professional matters, of course, has a noble position. Regardless of what phenomenal contributions a person has made, if he/she misbehaves once, such as cheating, lying, or committing fraud, he/she will tarnish his/her reputation badly and become the object of public criticism. People will tend to only remember this person's major fault, no matter what merits he/she possessed. To mend the destruction, this person might have to make more than ten times the effort to restore his/her stature.

My respect for reputation strengthens my self-discipline and compels me to conform to my code of conduct. Being decent and prudent can save me a tremendous amount of effort in remedying any misbehavior. Taking my reputation seriously is essential to me, as my upright image in the eyes of others is my invaluable intangible asset.

*List your qualities and strengths:

----

76. <u>To Be a Mind Reader</u>

If I want to be a good game player, first of all, I need to be a good observer and listener.

Observation helps me mature. By watching how people behave and listening to what they say, I learn about people's personalities and mentalities. From there, I consider how close of a relationship I should establish with them and how to interact with them, while I think and act in my own way without being affected by others. I know that other people do the same to me in a respectful way— they read my mind and evaluate me.

This practice is like playing chess. You are penetrating not only your rival's every single move, but also his/her entire scheme. In addition to what you can see on the surface, there is more underneath for you to figure out.

*Your thoughts:

Value of Time

77. <u>As Time Goes By</u>

The speed of time is uncontrollable. How much time a life has is unpredictable.

If you understand the value of time, you will not remain dispirited for too long after a break-up, because you will not want to waste too much of your precious time.

I view my life as a burning candle that will be extinguished one day. If I am lucky enough to live for one hundred years, every year I will burn off 1%; if I can live for seventy years, every year I will burn off about 1.5%. Unexpected things can happen at any moment—accidents, incidents, natural disasters, etc. There is a risk that my life could be forced to cease all of a sudden.

If I value my time, I will not commit myself to worthless things.

Therefore, throughout my life, I should continuously evaluate the productivity of my time.

*Perfectionism

I am not sure how many people have developed an obsession with perfection from their work, but I did. In practice, very often, finishing a task on time is better than spending excessive time getting it done perfectly. From time to time, when reviewing the performance of my projects, I have realized that I allocated too much time on insignificant matters. I was too obsessed with doing my job faultlessly, when I should have been more focused on the big picture rather than the small details.

I cannot get everything done flawlessly. The ability to let minor things go is essential in time management.

To clarify, efficiency does not mean sacrificing quality. On the contrary, efficiency assures excellence. Now, this world is already very developed and competitive. Countless brands, entities, and people are straining to fight against each other to stand out in the market. One's specialty is the secret weapon to win. Hence, one's focus should be optimizing his/her strongest point.

*Timing is key

Timing is a critical factor in reaching a goal. You will meet the right person at the right time. If the timing is wrong, even if everything else is a good fit, things may not work out in your favor.

How can I take advantage of the opportunities that arrive in front of me? Simply, when a favorable circumstance arises, do not hesitate.

As I mentioned, in the aftermath of my break-up, I was not shy about recording my feelings and thoughts, and this book is the by-product of the victory of defeating my misery. I would have never thought that I could write so outspokenly. If I were still working as an auditor for a well-known company, I would never have been so bold as to publish this survival experience, because I would have been cautious about upholding my professional image. Challenge and opportunity have an interesting relationship—I have found a way to turn this emotional storm into my motivation to write, which is like a spark inside a pile of hay with the promise to blaze into a roaring flame.

*The relationship between time and money

To enjoy a life in which I can devote my energy to fostering my potential, I must first establish a financial foundation. My lack of a stable income was the major reason why my previous two relationships failed.

Speaking realistically, without adequate money, I find it hard to make my self-value bloom, as I am spending most of my time and effort on satisfying my survival needs. With a sound financial base, I will be able to engage myself in the activities most beneficial to pursuing my passion.

As mentioned in Section 70, can money buy happiness? I believe, to a certain degree, it can. Some people say, "Money cannot buy you happiness, but it can buy you some time." I agree. Your time is limited. You can pay to get professional services in the areas with which you are not familiar in order to focus your time on the areas in which your talent lies.

Money is a resource to save time.

*Improving my time management

How to increase productivity is such a popular topic. In the first few years of my career, I labored under the over-optimistic belief that reaching all my objectives in one day would represent the highest productivity. Later, however, I not only had become exhausted from managing that heavy workload every day for a long period of time, but also ended up inefficient overall. Setting an overly intensive schedule was not helpful for time management. Draining myself to complete tasks aggressively was not a smart approach. After the unfavorable experiences of low efficiency, I have now realized that achieving my goals step-by-step, with balance in my body, mind, and soul, is the ideal strategy.

I do not have to be a workaholic to excel.

Methods to improve time management that I highly recommend:

1. Make your time visible: put plenty of clocks in your living and work spaces, so that you will not lose track of time. (Sounds funny, right? This is actually practical!)

2. Plan your schedule early enough: prepare short-term (daily) goals, as well as long-term (monthly/quarterly/yearly) goals in a to-do list, and prioritize the tasks. Avoid distractions. Concentrate! Concentrate! Concentrate!

3. Do significant things when your mind is in a good state: work on the most important tasks when your brain is the most active, mostly early in the day. Minor and repetitive tasks, which do not require you to think carefully, can be attended to when you are less energetic. Your prime time is limited, so make the most of it.

4. Reserve time for emergencies: give yourself enough breaks in your daily schedule. Unpredictable things come up all the time, so be prepared for emergent matters. Relaxation is also essential in your life. Do not forget to take time to regain your energy.

5. Avoid disturbances: put your phone on "silent" or "flight mode" to block out distractions when you really need to focus your time on one project, with an automatic response (your available time) on as a courtesy. Set alarms to alert yourself: "Get ready to wrap up!" and "Time is up!"

6. Record random ideas in time: jot down your thoughts whenever an idea flashes through your mind. Do not hesitate to write down notions that pop up suddenly, even your wild fantasy. Later, you can develop them when you have sufficient time.

7. Celebrate progress: reward yourself whenever you accomplish something, no matter how small. As you move forward and reach your milestones, counting every footprint along the way is highly encouraging and beneficial for the next phase.

78. How Efficient Are My 24 Hours?

Efficiency is the key to success.

Remain aware that efficiency may be easily affected by trivial matters. Have you ever experienced any of the following troublesome scenarios that can drive you crazy? All of them have happened to me:

a. I was getting ready for work in the morning, and I realized that I had forgotten to charge my phone, so there was only 10% battery left. My phone was dying.

b. The moment I closed the door, I realized that I had forgotten to take my key.

c. I went to a birthday party but forgot to bring the gift I had prepared.

d. I was on my way to an important meeting and got stuck in traffic. I had to get to my destination in ten minutes, but with the traffic, it would take me at least fifteen minutes. I felt like the whole world was burning!

e. I wanted to buy something, but I did not have enough cash or my credit/debit cards with me, and the store did not accept any mobile payment method. I ran a fruitless errand.

f. I thought that I had put my keys in a certain place, but I just could not find them.

g. I saw my USB flash drive many times, but then when I needed it, I could not find it.

h. I wanted to take a video with my phone, but it was out of memory.

i. One of my socks was missing.

j. I went to the kitchen and forgot what I was going to do.

k. I completely forgot to pay off my credit card bill for the last month.

l. I always intended to tidy up my desk, bookshelf, and wardrobe, but it just never happened.

m. I was handling too many messages in my e-mails and chat applications at the same time, and I forgot to reply to a few after reading them.

n. I stored an important document in a very safe place, and then I forgot where I had hidden it.

o. I found some money I had hidden a long time ago—nice surprise! It did cost me some time to look for it, though.

All of these situations brought me unnecessary hassles. A mess can waste a lot of my time and ruin my day.

Let me give you an example of how being organized can greatly benefit a person:

When I was a financial auditor, I was really impressed by one of the partners in our firm who had terrific organizational skills despite his heavy workload. He handled more than ten projects for large corporations simultaneously. I could imagine how busy his life was, but he always presented himself in a well-organized state. His office was always neat, tidy, and clear, even during peak seasons when most of us were immersed in mountains of files. His books were neatly placed on the bookshelf. There were no extra documents on his desk, but a pile of reports sat on the shelf behind him. A tall, verdant plant near the door and the city view in the window embellished the office perfectly.

He came to work earlier than most of the other employees. He could remember most of the important information about our clients after reviewing the reports and communicating with the teams. He could make decisions quickly after an efficient conversation with the team. He was never late for any meetings. Besides office work, he participated in the company's sports activities most Friday afternoons.

Generally, he was one of our role models.

One time, when I was working with this partner on a project, he came to my cubicle for a conversation about my assignment. When he saw my overwhelmed desk covered with piles of reports and files for different clients, he said to me, "Florence, you don't need so much."

He drove home the point that I should get my work environment more organized! I had been thinking about it for a long time without actually taking action. Thanks to his advice, I made up my mind to devote two hours to organizing my desk by putting everything in place. Also, I tidied up my computer files by explicitly naming them and locating them in the right folders. I felt wholly refreshed immediately following this reform!

After the betterment, my efficiency largely improved: I could find things easily; I could complete most of my plans on time; I rarely ran into a stressful moment.

The time I invested in organizing my stuff was worthwhile!

Sacrifice is not love.

My company does not need its employees to sacrifice themselves by spending most of their time on the job or being overwhelmed by work. My company needs people who can take care of their duties properly and efficiently.

In fact, not making an effort to improve my efficiency is a form of laziness.

A small habit may be a big deal in life.

Ten tips to become more organized in daily life:

1. Make your time noticeable: put plenty of clocks around you (as mentioned in the previous section).

2. Manage your library: organize the files and folders on your computer by naming them clearly to facilitate identification, showing the information such as document title, client name, update time, etc.

3. Organize your physical stuff: spend a few hours each month tidying up your paper documents, desk, shelf, and wardrobe. Place everything in a logical order. (It is funny that I often remind my friends to dispose of the expired food in their fridges!) For more suggestions on how to best achieve this, Marie Kondo, a tidying expert and bestselling author, gives good examples in her book *The Life-Changing Magic of Tidying Up*.

4. Set your schedule reasonably: put a to-do list with short-term and long-term goals in a visible place and update it regularly. Set reminders a few days before the due date for each task. Be realistic regarding your agenda, and do not try to accomplish too much at a time. Reserve time for rest. Break down a large project into different steps and mark your progress periodically. Check prices early enough if you need to book tickets.

5. Avoid disturbances: set a specific period of time as your "focus session" and politely let others know that you are working on a project exclusively during that time.

6. Back things up: make a backup of important files by sending them to your e-mail. Keep photos of important items, such as ID documents, on your phone so that they are handy, but be mindful of security!

7. Prepare your daily must-have items: put the things you need to take with you near the door so that you will not forget them when you leave.

8. Charge your phone in time: use a bright-colored cable for your phone charger and put it in a noticeable area.

9. Go to sleep early: enjoy quality sleep for at least seven hours each night. Take a nap when you feel tired during the day to refresh yourself.

10. Research online to get professional advice for specific issues. Do not spend too much time trying to figure everything out by yourself. Experts' recommendations and tips are widely available on the Internet nowadays.

Please also be reminded that being an early bird will always reward you!

Being organized will help you avoid a lot of frustrating moments and make your life much smoother. By conserving your time, you can be productive and set aside time to try new things to keep your days dynamic.

*Are there any areas in which you can further improve your time management?

----

79. The Words That Do Not Kill Me Can Rescue Me

When people tell us, "You are great just the way you are!" we are flattered, but I would rather hear people tell me, "This is not enough. You can do even better!" because this encouragement would motivate me to strive harder and achieve more. We should be appreciative of harsh yet honest comments, and even constructive criticism.

I believe that a little bit of external pressure can be helpful. I learned this during my fitness training class. One time, I asked the gym manager for advice regarding the pain that developed in my neck, shoulders, and back soon after working at my computer for a few hours, especially during those sleepless nights in the anguish caused by my break-up. He frankly said to me, "You don't really have muscles in your shoulders. You only have your skin, bones, and some lean meat in between." He explained to me that my muscles were not strong enough to support my body sitting in that position for a long time. It made sense to me, so I decided to enhance my body in those areas.

My physical trainer was very strict. During the first class, he told me to lift two eight-pound weights for an arm exercise. I bargained, "How about five pounds? Eight is too heavy for me." He replied, "You use the five ones when you do it by yourself. With me, eight." I had no choice but to follow his instructions. Later, he made me stay in a squat position for one full minute. I stood up ahead of time as my legs were sore. He commanded, "If you give up early next round, I will punish you with another two-minute squat." His serious look made me comply with all his orders.

When I was performing the challenging moves, only one conviction kept repeating in my head:

Compared to my break-up, this arduousness is nothing!

Ultimately, I finished the whole intensive thirty-minute session with a twisted and sweaty face. Right after that, my legs were trembling, but I felt amazingly relaxed and refreshed. I thanked him sincerely. He said to me, **"This is what you have paid me for."** Exactly! I did not make easy money. For sure, I paid him to train me, not to please me.

After being coached for a month, twice a week, half an hour each time, and surpassing my limit little by little in each session, I built up some muscles and lowered my fat ratio. The result was more evident than it would have been if I had worked out by myself. It propelled me to keep strengthening my body.

If I am confident enough, I am not afraid to hear others point out my weaknesses. On the contrary, I should be open to and thankful for the candid advice, which saves me time!

*Do people's comments and opinions bother you or help you?

----

80. The Days Spent with an Ex: Were They a Waste of Time?

Everyone's time is limited and precious, so we should spend it wisely. Were the days in which you had been with your ex considered worthless? Well, you did not know your efforts would be futile until that person became an ex. There is no point in feeling sorry for the time in hindsight.

When you are dating someone, you are holding out hope, either big or small, that the relationship may have a chance to bloom. There is nothing wrong with having hope.

I would say that my ex cost me time, not wasted my time. To perceive this in a positive light, a failed relationship can be construed as an investment in learning a lesson rather than a fruitless effort. We can definitely gain more wisdom from different failures during our lives. A person's ex(es) just help him/her mature.

You do not have to blame your ex for wasting your time. Blaming is not a solution. Time elapses in its own way no matter with whom you spend it. If the relationship cannot be salvaged, terminate it and move on to the next chapter of your life.

Here is a story about my friend Zoe leaving someone wrong for her and then finding someone right. She and her ex-boyfriend had dated for many years. After building their careers, the pair were about to get engaged. Unexpectedly, he told her that he was not yet ready for marriage. She was shocked. Knowing that this uncertain relationship would just consume more time, Zoe made up her mind and left him. Not long after the break-up, she found another man, a perfect match for her. They got married after dating for a few years, and since then they have been living happily together.

You and your ex can be great individuals but just not a good match together. Save the struggles for the rest of your life. Let it go. Let's play the next episode.

81. Do Not Let Obsession Cause You to Decay

I never used any drug to soothe myself after the break-up, because I can imagine how difficult it would be to beat addiction—extricating myself from my obsession with my ex has been disastrous enough. Since the break-up occurred, the withdrawal pain of knowing that I will not be with him again has been killing me. I absolutely do not want to experience another torment like this. I am even terrified of the thought of getting attached to someone or something.

In fact, obsession can develop unexpectedly. Be cautious of anything addictive. Here is my story to share—how I developed an obsession with social media.

Have you ever decided to go to sleep before eleven pm but then found yourself still browsing social media on your phone until after midnight? It has happened to me countless times.

There are so many fabulous people and interesting stories on the Internet. After I quit my job as an auditor, I wanted to be a songwriter and video creator, so I tried to keep up to date on the latest trends. As my mobile phone was always with me, I formed the habit of turning to social media every time I had a free moment. Gradually, I became glued to it.

Almost every night, I stayed up much later than I had planned because the first thing I did when I lay in bed was play with my phone. I could have finished browsing in five minutes, but I mostly ended up watching online content for more than an hour.

A lot of my time was consumed reading those nonessential yet amusing posts about other people's lives, such as gossip, rumors, pranks, jokes, silly fights, private matters, etc. It was fun to watch entertainment content, but it did not feed me what I needed. My energy was limited every day. I could have spent more of my precious time doing something useful for my future rather than viewing something irrelevant to my growth.

I have realized that this was a habit I slipped into unknowingly. Once an obsession is formed, it is very hard to quit. My experience has taught me that I should be able to notice an obsession with something quickly enough so that I can change my course of action before it is too late.

As for the matter of love, I should become cognizant of my excessive affection for a person before I sink too deep into a romantic flood. I do not want to hide anything from myself. I should be truthful with myself.

*Are you able to resist the temptation of something or someone?

Value of Health and Well-Being

82. <u>Miss Me After Losing Me?</u>

Youth is what everyone wants to retain, but we often mistreat it by the extravagant use of our bodies.

When I was in my teens and twenties, I studied and worked to the maximum regardless of the level of intensity my body could take. I slept for less than six hours a night during the week and only caught up on my sleep during the weekend. Sometimes I stayed up almost the entire night for work, parties, or watching my favorite TV programs, including the Olympic Games. At a young age, my energy could recover quickly by having a long sleep the following night.

However, since turning thirty, I feel different. The uninvited stiffness and pain in my neck, shoulders, and back from working at the computer often bother me. Moreover, my body does not recuperate as fast as before. Now it takes me a week to adapt to a ten-hour jet lag, while years ago I could overcome it in only two days. Sometimes I feel dizzy after working intensively. Every now and then, I just do not feel well, as if my body is not functioning for no reason.

Now I am aware that I have over-exploited my body and caused it to become impaired. Why I am anxious now: muscle tension disturbs me; my eyes have dark circles and pouches; I shed a lot of hair; I often feel fatigued; I gain weight easily; if I stay up late, I feel stress in my chest—I am only in my thirties, but I have already noticed the signs of aging that people usually develop around their fifties.

My aging is speeding up. If the decline of my body keeps up at this rate, I worry about whether I will be able to live to sixty years old. I am genuinely concerned!

In recent years, my body has given me many warnings. I love living in this magnificent world, but I understand that my splendid voyage will eventually end. I desire to prolong my life as much as possible, but I have not taken care of my health enough. My body has been worn out by my careless consumption.

Similarly, the body of our home, Earth, has been damaged by pollution in the water, soil, and air. Every inch of this land is invaluable to everyone. One day, if the situation becomes too severe to be remedied, it will be too late for humans to repent.

Life should be planned for the long term, not just the immediate benefit.

Nowadays, the pace of our lives is getting faster. People are constantly innovating to modernize the world. Things around us are changing rapidly. I feel that we are all striving to gain more time. I believe that if I can live ten years longer than average, I will be a winner!

I should put my health above my wealth. If my body is threatened by sickness, it will not matter how much I have in the bank, how luxurious my house is, or what a powerful title I hold. It may sound as though I have watched too many zombie-apocalypse movies, but in reality, my wellness indeed deserves my attention.

A car can be repaired by replacing the parts, but a person cannot be easily fixed in the same way. Actually, the human body has an amazing ability to recuperate by itself if a healthy routine is maintained. Nature has miraculously designed us.

As I explained in my reminiscence of how my beloved dog Shanelle passed away from an accident in Section 42 (Farewells to Our Pets), I now appreciate just how delicate life can be.

What would happen if I got sick and hopeless?

I imagined how people around me would react and how things would turn out if I were miserably ill and bedridden in the hospital:

- Mom would have to give up her comfortable life to take care of me all the time in the hospital, worrying, because she loves me unconditionally.

- My brother and sister would be financially stressed because I would be relying on my family and financial assistance from Social Security after using up my savings. Maybe they would have no alternative but to stop going on vacation. They would probably have arguments with their spouses over the troubles I brought on.

- My friends and colleagues would send me warm regards, which would be all they could give.

- My company would hire someone new to take over my position. The business deals I had created would start to make a handsome profit and my team would be celebrating with champagne and bonuses, without me.

- The man I adore would be dating or even marrying another woman.

- I would not invite anyone to visit me because I definitely would not want anyone to see me in this sorry state.

- I would be lying in bed in the hospital, probably with some machines connected to my body to sustain my life, watching my friends' posts on social media and learning about their enviable lives, which would no longer include me.

That would be the biggest nightmare I could ever have! Now, how can I allow myself to neglect my well-being?

Health is the foundation of life.

Love yourself by loving your health first!

83. <u>Aging, Please Slow Down!</u>

Under the impact of my break-up, I looked horrible. Thanks to those sleepless nights, when I looked in the mirror, I saw an aged woman. I told myself, "You are SO OLD NOW!"

I looked ten years older in just one week following the break-up. The heavy dark circles under my eyes, the pimples on my forehead, my puffy face, my dull skin ... I was amazed by how much I had deteriorated due to just one emotion attack.

You know how much effort it takes to maintain one's beauty, right? However, I lost it instantly from a bloody break-up—this was such a bad deal!

Here, I would like to emphasize that it requires persistence in following a strict lifestyle to slow down aging, but a break-up can accelerate aging dramatically! I must take action to stop this adverse consequence.

Sadness is the No. 1 killer of beauty!

Happiness is the critical element to "freeze" a person's age, with self-discipline coming second. Fortunately, this break-up has not devoured me because I have disciplined myself even more rigorously since it occurred. I have witnessed the course of transformation in myself, from an overnight collapse to complete recovery. I am gratified that I have finally survived this break-up. I have also learned that one's determination is key to slowing down the aging process.

84. <u>Evergreen</u>

Do I genuinely know the person in front of me in the mirror? What I have learned from some specialists' studies is that sometimes what I see in the mirror does not precisely reflect reality—as if the mirror lies.

My brain sometimes plays tricks on my vision to help me see myself the way I prefer rather than the way I truly am. My brain can covertly adjust the sight of my flaws. In other words, my brain can obscure my imperfections. That is why sometimes I am surprised that the me in photographs does not look as appealing as the person I see in the mirror. This may be due to my brain, the lighting, the angle, or the quality of the camera. For example, my face is not symmetrical (one side is a bit larger than the other), but this is not obvious to me when I look in the mirror. When I look at my pictures, though, I can tell right away.

After this break-up, I looked at myself in the mirror carefully, trying to exclude any bias. I understood that the emotional challenge, life stress, and aging had severely affected me. I could tell from a lot of symptoms: poor memory, aches in my muscles, wrinkles, hair loss, heavy eye bags, and taking more time to overcome jet lag. These physical conditions were hard to reverse, and I would never go back to being eighteen years old, the age at which I could rehabilitate myself in a short time.

I should be courageous enough to acknowledge this fact:

I cannot defy aging, so I have to preserve myself.

We know that moderate exercise can keep us young, but we always come up with "convenient" excuses to evade it. Have you ever said the following to yourself (I have)?

- I am too busy working and have no time to build my body.
- I am so heartbroken that I do not feel my strength.

- Let me finish this project first; then, I will make time.
- Let me finish this episode; then, I will go.
- The weather does not look suitable today.

If you do not want to do it, no one can force you. If you earnestly intend to do it, no one can stop you. It all depends on your drive. It is just like when you have a crush on someone, no one, not even yourself, can stop you from thinking about that person.

At the beginning of the break-up, a part of me was still unable to accept the fact that our story was finished. I was silly enough to hold onto the wishful thought that if I could manage to live for another fifty years, maybe he would come back to me one day.

Certainly, I should try to live nicely for another fifty years, but not for him. I aspire to enjoy a long and high-quality life. I do not want to grow old or see my physique decline. I imagine you feel the same, don't you?

Either as revenge upon him or as a favor to myself, I have resolved to do my best to slow down my aging. I have been pretty strict with myself and right now I affirm to myself:

Stay young or fall!

This is my resolution because the break-up was such a stab in my heart, as I mentioned in Chapter III (Revealing My Dark Side). The pain has been the impetus for me to renovate myself.

As for anti-aging, first of all, what makes people age more quickly than usual? My answer: sadness, lack of sleep, and an unbalanced diet. Thus, I have to avoid all of these detrimental factors that steal my well-being.

The following are ten things I regularly do to keep myself energetic, in light of my research and personal experience. I hope that they can be a helpful reference for you:

1. Get enough sleep

   Go to bed before midnight and ensure that you enjoy at least seven hours of quality sleep every night. It is best to follow the sun's schedule.

2. Nap

   Take a nap during the day for ten to thirty minutes after lunch or when you feel exhausted. A snooze is an efficient way to recharge yourself.

3. Moderate exercise

   Exercise (at a suitable level in accordance with your physical condition) at least one hour each day, three times per week. Attending a dance class and jogging are good options. An extra benefit of dancing is that learning the dance moves trains your brain.

4. Perspiration

   Sweat at least three times a week, ideally through exercise.

5. Watch your diet

   Take everything in moderation—balance in nutrition from natural food. Avoid too many artificial ingredients. Resist the temptation to eat unhealthy yet tasty food (I know this is hard, but you will definitely see the benefits after quitting them!). Drink enough water!

6. Relax

   Do something to calm yourself down at least once a week. Singing, which I find to be one of the most relaxing activities, can be done anywhere and at any time.

7. Meaningful conversation

   Talk to someone wise once a month. Candidates can be your family members, friends, schoolmates, teachers, mentors, and co-workers. An inspiring conversation nourishes your mind!

8. Release your emotions

   Cry when emotions surge up within you: find a quiet place, be alone, and shed tears. If they want to come, let them come.

9. Replenish yourself with dopamine

   Laugh very hard once a week by talking with someone about silly things or watching funny videos. Make sure to laugh hard enough, even to the point of bursting into tears.

10. Back to basics

   Periodically enjoy your time in a more "natural" state—for example, eat light, stay away from electronic devices, spend some time in nature (parks, hills, or beaches), and wear less makeup.

In general, follow nature's design!

According to common wisdom, a peaceful mind is the key to longevity. You look radiant when you smile from your heart!

*List your practices for enhancing your health:

Value of Forgiveness

85. <u>Loss or Gain?</u>

Reviewing my break-up in hindsight, I felt like my willpower attended a merciless training course, where my soul revived through combating anguish, frustration, and depression.

I fell really hard, as if the break-up had pushed me off a cliff. I was stranded in despair. The bitterness enslaved me for more than a year. However, instead of remaining stagnant and negative, I endured the pain, proactively moved forward, and finally rebooted my life.

Thanks to my break-up as the stimulus, an uplifted version of me was born, because I turned the fury of my grief into momentum in every facet of my life:

- Physically:

  I released my rage at my fitness classes, where my tears and sweat were mixed. Within a year, the improvement of my body was apparent: I built muscles and even felt that my footsteps were lighter; I could run faster; I became more energetic; my skin looked brighter. My friends and colleagues were impressed by my transformation. They attributed it to my new career, but actually, my break-up was the trigger of the changes.

- Mentally:

  To optimize my precious time, I purified my mind and organized my belongings to improve my efficiency. What is more, I have become much better at controlling my emotions. I have found balance in my life again.

- Career-wise:

  Besides my primary occupation, I have been embracing my enthusiasm for creative writing, so now I feel passionate every day.

Was the break-up a loss or a gain for me? In reality, it could have been both, but I kept "brainwashing" myself into believing that it was definitely not a loss, but absolutely a GAIN!

Are you afraid of falling in love again? You might be if you have ever failed at it. Nevertheless, once you have triumphed over that failure with your strength, you will be amazed by how much you have gained!

*List the achievements you have made after battling your emotional struggles:

----

86. Forgiveness Is the Greatest Gift

Forgiving someone is probably the hardest thing to do. To forgive is to let go of someone's mistake and move on. Forgiveness is the ultimate form of generosity.

If I were forgiven for what I have done wrong, it would be priceless to me.

Knowing that time is valuable, I try to let trifling things go right away. If someone is late for our meeting or causes me a small loss, I simply let it go because such trivial matters do not substantially affect my life. I am not inclined to waste my time and energy blaming someone for small errors. On the other hand, understanding that it is not easy for some people to forgive others, I always try to avoid hurting anyone.

It requires one's greatest efforts to earn others' forgiveness. To this day, there is only one person I have not come to forgive: my father, who abandoned my family when my siblings were very young. He has been absent from my life for more than twenty years. I have tried to expel him from my memory. I do not now, and probably never will, welcome him back into my life. I have asked myself many times, "When will I bury the hatchet and finally be on good terms with him again?" Honestly, I still do not feel ready for that, despite the fact that he and I are bonded by blood.

Forgiveness is one of the greatest virtues.

The break-up with my ex left me sad and disappointed for more than a year. I blamed myself for being so foolish. I was ashamed of myself for being such a feeble person. In spite of the hardship, gradually, and with tremendous effort, I have walked out of the darkness.

I have acknowledged that even if I could go back in time, there would not be much I could change to achieve a better result.

I have come to understand that it is meaningless to look to the past, entangled in pessimism. Instead, a positive attitude is the motor that drives me forward.

Finally, I forgave myself for obsessing over a romantic relationship, and it was the biggest present I gifted to myself this year!

87. Would You Get Back Together with Your Ex?

Right before I finished writing this book, I wanted to add one more section:

What about getting back with your ex?

By the time I completed this book, I did not want to go back to my ex. Still, I could not predict how I might feel in five, ten, or thirty years from now. What if I change my mind?

My break-up is a wound that has not yet healed completely, and I understand that the scar will always remain, just like a fracture in cracked glass. When I look back at my break-up, or think of him involuntarily, it still feels like acid is being poured over a cut.

So, here is a question for you:

After your break-up, if your ex comes to apologize and asks for forgiveness, will you get back together with him/her?

You may be scared of loving that person again, or you may still be optimistic. Making the same mistake may not be smart, but you cannot discount the possibility that the relationship can be improved this time. If one day you want to allow your ex to enter your life again, why not give both of you a chance? Worst-case scenario: you might go through another "break-up rehab."

Perhaps you are truly over your ex now. If so, congratulations! You have embarked on a brand-new voyage of amassing the treasure of happiness! Do not miss out on anything valuable in this world. There are so many wonderful people and fantastic things out there for you to discover.

When a girlfriend asked me, "Should I give him another chance?" I told her, "Please think about what you stand to gain and what you might lose by taking another chance with him. If he only hurt you once and is willing to improve the situation, you may give the relationship another shot. However, if he has wronged you many times and will not amend the problem, what kind of benefit are you going to get by trying one more time? Maybe it is time that you offer yourself a chance to sever yourself from the past and set yourself free. Anyhow, if you want to welcome him back into your life, letting bygones be bygones, just follow your heart. Be reminded that a reunion should be on the premise of a deal—mutual respect."

As long as you are strong enough to survive any break-up, you can be brave enough to try or restart a romantic adventure.

Life is a process—learning, growing, and enjoying. Just fill every chapter of your journey with fabulous stories!

*Your thoughts:

Now,

are you ready to embrace the brand-new version of yourself?

Chapter XV Let Go

88. The Real Me Is Back, with Glory!

As time passed, our love story evaporated. All I can do is let go.

Honestly, I am not sure whether I have fully gotten over him, but I have survived this break-up. How can I tell? Now, my feelings toward the history of my ex and me do not impact my judgment in my life; the memories of him no longer cause me sleepless nights; even when he appeared in my dreams occasionally, my emotions were not seriously affected. Although he holds a special place in my heart, it is not hurtful anymore. The recollections of him are now like ripples, which do not give rise to dangerous waves. I can just respect it as one segment of my past.

During the first six months following the break-up, I went out to social events a lot to make new friends. I met five bachelors, kind people, but I did not end up dating any of them. Maybe I was too picky; perhaps I was very cautious; my mind was probably still burdened; I was possibly not good enough … or I just had not encountered the right man yet. Although I did not fall for any of these men, they impressed me with their attributes and heartened me by showing that there was hope out there.

Then, I paused on dating and have been contentedly focusing on my career for more than a year. The conflict between different voices in my heart has ceased. Slowly, my pain has subsided, and hopefully, it will vanish entirely one day. Progressively, I have let the past flow away.

I believe that recovering from my heartbreak has elevated my soul to another level. Time heals. All I need is a firm belief in myself. I have lost him already. I must not lose myself.

Since the break-up, I have been thinking about myself, my past, and my future. I keep deliberating on the meaning of living in this world. Comprehending the worth of my existence for a finite time, I have endeavored to revitalize myself to embrace my brand-new world!

As I have mentioned several times, when an adverse circumstance befalls a person, EQ plays a leading role in his/her life. I should learn to surmount a challenge with an optimistic attitude and **turn my tragedy into a comedy**. Now, reviewing my survival in hindsight, I can be candid with myself that I was once a besotted girl, like many other people.

I endorse my determination to improve myself physically and mentally in response to my break-up. I am proud of my breakthrough in managing my emotions. Now, even if the whole world except me were in love, I would be just fine being single, because I am confident enough in living a fulfilling life alone, as well as in my faith that I will eventually find a significant other.

I have buried that piece of my history of being immature, sentimental, and fragile.

I feel like I am immune to temptation.

I will not be manipulated by pheromones.

I have transformed my heart from a crystal into a diamond.

Who can break me, again?

Enslaved by the affection I had for him for years before the break-up, I had been unhappy because I felt lost. I am glad that I realized where I lost myself, so I knew how to find *her*.

I lost that relationship, but I found myself.

Now, I am back, with a beaming smile!

Chapter XVI   Thank You for Reading!

In this final chapter, I would like to thank you for reading my book, even just a few pages, a couple of sentences, or simply the cover—my sincere gratitude to you!

This book is a journal about my wound, my pain, and my scar, as well as my insights from my arduous journey through healing.

The biggest reward for me is that my experiences and understanding shared in this book have accompanied you and consoled you through your challenging time. It means so much to me that my book has also inspired you to 1) think and act more rationally and optimistically, and 2) write down your own thoughts and reasoning regarding emotional matters to come up with the best solutions for yourself—these are my purposes of writing this book. Hopefully, it has served you effectively!

Any feedback, questions, comments, likes, agreements, disagreements, criticism, etc. are all very welcome! Please let me know on:

Instagram or Twitter: @florencesbook

In summary, my break-up has helped me understand that:

- Heartbreak is no fun! I cried, struggled, and admitted it.
- Break-ups happen in the course of a lifetime. It is all right.
- I keep learning from everything, as life is a process.

I trusted myself. I let go. I am boldly moving on.

Now, I feel LIBERATED!

Thank you!

I am looking forward to hearing from you!

Acknowledgments

I want to express my gratitude to:

The first group of reviewers of this book: Jy Prishkulnik, Beverly Hindin, Caroline Juchniewicz, Daniel Wilson, and Diane Fraze. I sincerely appreciate your honest and valuable comments!

Mom, thank you for bringing me into this world! You have raised me with abundant love and care, as well as educated me to be a diligent and upright person. Besides being a role model for me, you have encouraged me to comprehend the worth of a life and be the master of my future. Nothing makes me feel better than appreciating the process of pursuing all kinds of value during my existence. Being a part of this fascinating planet is my greatest luck.

My friends, thank you all for being supportive along the way. Wisdom, kindness, and generosity are what I see in you. I am so fortunate to have you in my life.

My dark side, your presence was the best remedy for my emotional crisis. You gave me the power to fix my heart, my feelings, my emotions, my attitude, and my life.

Lastly, thank you to my ex. Thank you for everything you have taught me, and for giving me the opportunity to learn to become a brave warrior.

References

YouTube Videos

Jay Shetty. (2018, April 3). *If They Left You - WATCH THIS | by Jay Shetty.* Retrieved from:
http://www.youtube.com/watch?v=hBVX5s43_Ks

Meghan Trainor. (2015, July 10). *Meghan Trainor - Like I'm Gonna Lose You (Official Music Video) ft. John Legend.* Retrieved from:
https://www.youtube.com/watch?v=2-MBfn8XjIU

Films

Black Swan. Directed by Darren Aronofsky, performance by Natalie Portman, Cross Creek Pictures, 2010.

Alita: Battle Angel. Directed by Robert Rodriguez, performance by Rosa Salazar, 20th Century Fox, 2019.

Books

Behrendt, Greg, and Liz Tuccillo. *He's Just Not That Into You: The No-Excuses Truth to Understanding Guys.* New York: Simon Spotlight Entertainment, 2004.

Kondo, Marie. *The Life-Changing Magic of Tidying Up: The Japanese Art of Decluttering and Organizing.* New York: Ten Speed Press, 2014.

Postscript:

<u>Notes for the days faced with a novel coronavirus</u>

Not long before this book's release (04/04/2020), many countries around the world started taking actions to confront the threat of COVID-19. Sad news has been reported every day. Some people lost their lives, while many others lost their loved ones. At this moment, no one can forecast when the pandemic will be controlled worldwide. The primary goal for the year 2020 for a lot of people, including me, is: **staying alive**.

During this crisis, we can see many different sides of our society:

- Most of us have remained prudent and followed the orders from the authorities to keep ourselves in self-quarantine or a social-distancing state because we do not want to take a chance and increase the burden on our communities. Still, some people acted of their own accord and refused to comply.
- We cannot give enough appreciation and praise to the doctors, nurses, and other personnel working on the front lines to rescue patients, despite the risk of getting infected. They are true heroes! Meanwhile, some people used this crisis as an opportunity to make money dishonestly.
- What is more frightening is that we have seen some unverified news, exaggerated reports, radical opinions, negative attitudes, and concealment on mass media.
- Yet, there is something gratifying—pollution in our air and water has been largely reduced in many cities due to the pause in a lot of business activities as a result of the self-quarantine. We can imagine how many harmful things we have done to nature.

From this tough period we are all going through, I would like to express two points of view:

1) The choice of my attitude is up to me.

At the beginning of this critical time, some people were unhappy about self-quarantine and social distancing, which are the best ways to prevent the spread of the virus before a vaccine becomes available. Instead of positively supporting the actions to cope with the situation, some media posted videos of empty streets with sad music, which created a sense of desolation, and some people showed how boring life was without social events.

I think negative attitudes like these are inappropriate. In fact, people can continue their lives effectively and productively under quarantine. We can work and study at home, collaborate through the Internet, enjoy family time, have phone calls with our relatives and friends, learn what we like, practice healthy cooking, organize our stuff, etc. No matter where we are, time is just valuable, so we have to make use of it. We should learn to be adaptable because there can be unexpected rain or even storms in our lives at any time. Under a life-threatening circumstance, we need optimism, compassion, flexibility, discipline, and solidarity. We should also stay clearheaded regardless of unhealthy reports and remarks around us.

2) My body deserves to be taken care of.

When a virus presents itself and endangers our lives, it is our immune system that clears the virus and saves ourselves, before an effective remedy is developed. People with compromised health conditions tend to be more vulnerable when facing disease. Maintaining one's health requires continuous effort, including sufficient sleep, a balanced diet, moderate exercise, a happy mood, and a positive attitude.

A life is such a miracle, but it is so delicate at the same time. Compared to a lethal disease, a break-up is definitely insignificant. Remember, health guarantees the feasibility of the next romantic adventure. Each of us is granted one precious opportunity to live his/her life to the fullest in this world, and this opportunity comes with both the rights and obligations to love oneself first and then others.

Best wishes to us all!

March 26, 2020
Florence Chow

MORE OF YOUR IDEAS:

MORE OF YOUR IDEAS: